# SEX

## AND
## THE
## CHRISTIAN
## TEEN,
## 101

# SEX

## AND THE CHRISTIAN TEEN, 101

**TOM WATSON, Jr.**

**BAKER BOOK HOUSE**
Grand Rapids, Michigan 49516

Copyright 1989 by Baker Book House Company

ISBN: 0-8010-9694-4

*Second printing, September 1989*

Printed in the United States of America

This one's for

**Katy**
**David**
**Josh**
**Lolly**
**Jesse**
**Suzanne**
and
**Katheryn**

who now face the challenge of life
in a tough and tempting world,
while proving the truth and merit
of what this book is all about.

# Contents

# Introduction

As your body and mind develop, sexual feelings and desires likely influence much of what you think and do. If you accept responsibility for these feelings and desires, learn to keep them under control, and use them in the way God intended, they can enhance your zest for the good and happy life.

But we all know that not everyone owns up to that responsibility, maintains that control, or respects God's purposes. Those people soon discover that misunderstood sexual feelings and misused desires can cause frustration, embarrassment, misery, fear, pain, disease, and even untimely death.

It is important that you learn now how to understand your sexuality, that you come to terms with it so as to use those powerful forces inside your body and mind to the best possible advantage. Wise use of your sexuality will leave you with few regrets and a whole lot of joy. Misuse of it can rob sex of all the good things and make it a threat—not only for you but also for others who share your world.

Did God actually invent teenagers? Yes, he did! Adolescence is a process God intended all humans to endure. The teen years represent a high-pressured growth stage, a time for taking giant steps toward maturity. To a large degree, you should be allowed—as I was—to make a few mistakes and learn from your experiences. One day you and your peers will rule the world, but only after you have survived your teen years and young adulthood, endured a whole lot of setbacks, overcome obstacles, and acquired an enormous amount of knowledge. All of that means you have wisely developed the potential planted within you at birth.

You will be able to acquire a lot of that "survival training" on your own. But some areas of knowledge are best acquired from outside sources that are wise, friendly, and reliable. At the top of that list of special topics is the old bugaboo called "sex."

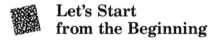 **Let's Start from the Beginning**

Acquiring reliable knowledge about sex from wise and friendly sources is what a book like this is all about. That's why we will start from the beginning:

- All humans and other animals come into the world as babies.
- All baby humans and other animals develop from eggs.

- Animal pairings produce offspring that are the same species as the parents. This implies "no trespassing" sexually between species.
- All humans and other animals are either male or female. Boys and girls grow up to be either men or women and then become (if healthy) capable of reproducing their own children. This process ensures the continuation of each species upon this earth.

Simple facts, right? Of course, but a few years ago you didn't know even these basics. Since they are typical statements right out of sex-education materials, it seems a reasonably good place for us to begin. We were not born with an instinctive awareness of things like that. Someone had to tell us, and preferably the telling is done by someone who really knows and cares and can be trusted to give us the whole truth.

In the realm of sex, too many myths and half-baked truths surround you to take a chance on being misinformed or defrauded. The land mines and bear traps along the path to acquiring sex information can hurt you more than help you, and they can inflict emotional scars that will plague you the rest of your life. In fact, your view of sex right now could be both confused and dangerous.

##  The Basics and Beyond

"Sex" and "sexuality" are words that refer broadly to the intimate organs of the body, including the pleasure and excitement we get from them. But the subject extends far beyond bedroom fun-and-games. That popular three-letter word—SEX—is not just a guy and a gal stirring up erotic feelings. It covers a lot of territory beyond the basic facts about birds and bees, birth control, and avoiding disease.

In textbooks, "sex" is defined as the physical difference that distinguishes organisms according to their function in the reproductive process. That sounds boringly scientific, but it is the proper place for people to begin their search for truth and reality about sex.

### Primary-Sexual Differences

Biologically, humans and animals and most plants are classified by their primary sexual characteristics as "male" or "female." Males produce spermatozoa; females produce ova. At the basis of the whole process is the difference between the sperm and the egg. The internal or external sex organs of plants, humans and other animals, are related to that difference. Those organs are designed to manufacture and either transmit or receive what is required for the species to reproduce itself.

### Secondary Sexual Differences

The colorful plumage on a male bird, the male lion's mane, and the crowing of a rooster are all secondary sexual differences. So (when comparing "averages") is a man's deeper voice, his greater height, his beard, his more highly developed muscular structure, and his eventual tendency toward balding. In contrast to that is a woman's higher-pitched voice, her breast development, and her rounded hips. All that, too, comes under the category of "sex." To furnish a worthwhile educational experience, a book on the subject of sex needs to examine the secondary differences as well as the primary and discover why they are part of the master plan.

But that isn't all you need to know.

### *Values and Priorities*

A sex-education book should also talk about values and priorities, even though some people may fail to see their relevance to sexuality. Ignorance about the basic "facts of life" can cause a lot of pain and regret, but confusion about values and priorities can cause even more. Mere knowledge and experience in the physical realm of sex without a set of proven values and priorities can make an otherwise worthwhile and intelligent young person a sitting duck for personal disaster.

This book can make you a luckier duck than that.

Setting priorities and establishing values, by the way, is not just a religious exercise. Those principles are not something the church or the Bible presses on us, whether we like it or not. They are not just some theologian's ideas of "good" and "bad," or "moral" and "immoral." What most sexual values and priorities boil down to is common sense and survival, and that comes through knowledge, understanding, and learning from the right kind of experience at the right time.

 ## Tying the Loose Ends

This book can help you pull a lot of loose ends together so they will make sense. Don't be surprised if you find information here you knew already. That is to be expected. Unless you have been living in a vacuum all these years, your natural instincts and curiosity have led you into adventures from which you learned a great deal. But there is more you ought to know—and some of what you think you know is not that way at all. That faulty information can hurt you a lot.

I believe you will make some happy and worthwhile discoveries on the pages that follow, and I'm grateful and glad you are reading my book.

# 1

## Ferdinand on Fatherhood*

Ferdinand is far more intelligent than many living creatures at his age and station in life. Besides that, if his figures can be trusted, at last count he had fathered an incredible 53 children who had, in turn, produced for him 165 grandchildren, 431 great-grandchildren and. . . . Well, there is really no merit in continuing our research into Ferdinand's sexual prowess. The point, it seems, has been proven.

*Some readers may feel the author's selection of a dog denigrates the responsibility aspect of fatherhood. However, the illustration is intended to demonstrate that, unlike animals, humans have been "fearfully and wonderfully made" in God's image and are indeed responsible to him not only for their own behavior but also for the effects of that behavior on others.

## His Numbers
## Are Not Reliable

One reason we can stop counting is that Ferdinand
himself is not sure about the numbers. He keeps re-
calling other almost-forgotten encounters that might
also have produced offspring. The statistics remain in-
complete and unreliable. Nevertheless, Ferdinand's ac-
complishments are so impressive that his observations
on fatherhood might warrant a prominent place in this
book about sex—though not, perhaps, for the reasons
*he* might assume.

Ferdinand's remarkable intelligence adds much to his
credibility in this vital area. To make the picture complete, I am including here a list of the unusual feats
that distinguish him from most of his peers. Ferdinand
can shake hands, roll over, play dead, and bark on com-
mand. He can jump through a hoop, walk on his hind
legs, and bring in the morning newspaper. Unfortunately, he has not yet learned to read it, but that would
be expecting a lot from a dog.

That single flaw, however, need not lessen the value
of Ferdinand's testimony. If he could speak his mind
about the joys of the act that has made him a father so
many times, this is probably what he would say:

> Mating is more fun than fetching sticks, catching
> frisbees, or even chasing cars down Figtree Street.
> Sometimes it seems to have the edge even on eating.
> Fathering puppies is something I can do anywhere, any
> time, and with anybody who passes two simple tests:
> she's got to be a girl and she's got to be in the mood.
>     Fortunately for me, I live in the city where girls in

the mood are not hard to find. Some dogs I know insist that life on the farm is better because they've got more territory available. But I don't buy that—there's too little variety down on the farm. In the city where I live there must be ten dogs to every block, and half of them are girls. The only possible problem I could think of would be if all of them got in the mood at the same time!

Whenever I speak out on this subject, some killjoy is sure to bring up the matter of consequences, so I'll cover that before we go any further. Fatherhood does involve puppies, of course. There was a time early in my adventures when I didn't understand that, but I soon got educated about the facts of life. Where there is sex, there will be puppies. It's a male's world, though, and puppies definitely are a mother's responsibility. Whoever saw a self-respecting father curled up in a doghouse, letting a litter of puppies crawl all over his stomach?

It does make a guy feel important to know that the town is full of kids he brought into the world. And don't rely on the numbers Mr. Watson gave you at the beginning of this chapter. Remember, he's only a human, and humans probably don't understand how difficult it is to tell which puppies are mine and which are the results of some other mongrel's fun-and-games. I just gave him my best guess because he kept asking.

My philosophy doesn't let me worry too much about details like that. If I did, I might have a conscience problem about making puppies with my daughters or granddaughters—or maybe with my own mother.

You want to know how I feel about females? If they're big enough, they're old enough. If they're in the mood— and I can always tell—they're fair game. I don't worry about sentiment, conscience, or love. These human ideas

would only complicate matters. After all, we're not setting up housekeeping. We're just having good, clean fun.

## Things a Dog Can't Understand

Thank you, Ferdinand. Our young readers will find that most enlightening, if not admirable by human standards.

Since Ferdinand is not particular about where he does his mating, you may have seen him or some of his pals in action somewhere in your neighborhood. If you have, what you saw requires a few words of explanation. First, in spite of Ferdinand's intelligence, he could never qualify for medical school, so there are many details he doesn't understand. Perhaps—like you, for example— he never heard of "an estrus cycle." That term describes a series of regular biological changes that all female animals, including humans, go through. The changes are controlled by the production of female hormones and are a necessary part of the reproduction process. The estrus cycle is programmed into the genes of every female through a mysterious coding system that provides convincing evidence of a Master Designer who is responsible for the whole idea. The adult female's ability to produce children comes around as regularly as clockwork, but the time periods involved are different in every species.

Ferdinand, of course, does not need to know the scientific explanation of the estrus cycle. What he really needs to know is the smell a female dog gives off when she's "in heat." His sense of smell is all it takes to motivate him to the sexual activity that can make him a father.

Ferdinand's girl friends come into heat once or twice a year and stay that way for about a week. Only during that time do their ovaries deposit eggs in their uterus, or "womb." It is during estrus that female dogs will allow sexual activity to take place.

 ## The Mating Game

Ferdinand's keen sense of smell keeps him posted on the moods of all the girls in his neighborhood. When they are "ready," so is he. With his first sniff of that special smell, his penis swells and comes out of its protective skin covering. His mating instincts go into action. He zeroes in on his target and tries to climb on the female's back. If she cooperates, he manages to make the necessary insertion, and the puppy factory is in full operation.

With each encounter, however, there's a surprise in store for Ferdinand, although he probably forgets about it from one conquest to the next. At the base of his penis is something called a bulbourethal gland that swells dramatically after it is inserted. Before Ferdinand ejaculates and deposits several million male spermatozoa in the female, the gland has become so big that it can't move back through his partner's vagina. So they are stuck in what would be described by most humans as an embarrassing situation.

Outraged owners of female dogs that they don't want made pregnant have squirted the hose on a Ferdinand and chased him with sticks, but to no avail. In that situation, male dogs usually manage to get one leg over the female's hip and turn around, so the two dogs stand there helplessly, tail to tail. Almost nothing can separate them until the gland shrinks enough ten to fifteen minutes later to be withdrawn from the vaginal opening.

About sixty-three days after mating is accomplished, Ferdinand has another litter of puppies to his credit. The mother, however, inherits the total responsibility for their care and feeding.

##  Unless He Learns to Read . . .

Some important lessons can be learned from Ferdinand's hypothetical observations—which is the reason they are included in this book. But unless he learns to read and could understand what I've written, I advise you to take his recommendations with a grain of salt. Furthermore, we know that in countless ways a human being is not "just another animal."

# 2

# Millicent on Motherhood*

If you are a girl, it is hardly necessary to warn you that a great gulf is fixed between you and Millicent, the lady I am going to quote theoretically in this chapter. It would be difficult—no, downright impossible—for either of you to cross that gulf. Still, if she were able to, Millicent would probably insist on sharing with you her insights and feelings about sexuality and parenthood. I would not have the heart to deny her that privilege. Who knows? You might benefit from hearing about her frequent experiences in the realm of motherhood.

*Some readers may feel the author's selection of a cow denigrates the concept of motherhood. However, the illustration is intended to demonstrate that, unlike animals, humans have been "fearfully and wonderfully made" in the image of God and are indeed responsible to him not only for their own behavior but also for the effects of that behavior on others.

Millicent weighs approximately 750 pounds—considerably more, I trust, than you do. How else is she different from you? She wears no clothes, has four legs and two horns, and eats mostly grass, grain, and silage.

You're right, Millicent is a cow. As you read, don't forget that gulf I mentioned.

Since Millicent considers Ferdinand's comments in the previous chapter outrageously chauvinistic, she is demanding equal time. I am a bit embarrassed by that because this was planned to be a book that creates no unnecessary controversy. Still, everyone is entitled to his or her opinion, and my publisher insists it is better to keep everything open and aboveboard in a book about sex. Mothers everywhere have a right to be heard.

 ## She Started Early in Life

Millicent's experiences as a mother began phenomenally "early" by human standards. She nursed her first baby before she was three years old. If that is surprising, bear in mind that by the time Millicent is as old in actual years as you are, she won't be able to have children any more. When she reaches fifteen she will most likely be—forgive the morbid thought—dead.

Millicent's bovine molecular structure is the reason for the gulf I've been talking about. And all those differences between cattle and humans are the reasons she must learn in a hurry whatever she needs to know about sex. No doubt you will keep all that in mind as you read what Millicent might candidly contribute on the sacred subject of motherhood:

> It is my personal opinion that mothers are, by and large, victims of male ego and their own physiology.

Bulls are the villains, and the biological computers built into all cows are accessories to the crime. The way I look at it, motherhood is just another gigantic conspiracy in the hands of a male-dominated universe.

I don't recall any bull ever asking me for my opinion on the subject of sex, or, for that matter, asking my permission to take advantage of me. Everything about sex seems so—well, so mechanical. At an early age I discovered I was equipped with a biological computer that triggers my sexual responses and takes matters out of my own hands. Or should I say hoofs? The same thing is true of my girl friends. We're victims all. Sooner or later, all of us wake up one morning to the realization that we cows are controlled by a timeclock. Ferdinand already referred to something you humans call our "estrus."

I didn't ask for this cycle. I didn't even get to program the computer. One day I was a young heifer and standing there in a nice patch of clover, grazing and minding my own business. Suddenly, gently but firmly, something turned me on. Until that moment, sex had meant nothing. If some bull in my pasture had gotten fresh, I would have kicked his teeth in. But, when my computer kicked in its make-a-baby program, I couldn't think about anything but sex for several days.

Once it got started, the cycle kept happening with frustrating regularity. It still puts me on a twenty-one–day merry-go-round. For three weeks I couldn't care less about bulls and their preoccupation with love-making. But every time that fourth week rolls around, I become—let me tell you—a real animal for a few days.

You want to know what my human owner's book on animal husbandry has to say about that? It makes it sound awfully technical and impersonal, but since you readers are human, it's probably worth remembering: "The egg of the cow develops in a fluid-filled sac called

a follicle, which is located in the ovary. The follicle secretes estrogen into the bloodstream, and this causes changes in the animal's behavior."

Changes? You'd better believe it! When my estrogen turns that computer on, I'm a different woman. For something like eighteen hours, that egg is in just the right place and just the right position in my female apparatus, and that's when my computer sounds the mating call. I would really like to be more selective, but I just seem to lose control. Any old bull will do, and at that point I'm not the least concerned about having any privacy for our lovemaking. The bull deposits about fourteen billion male sperm in my uterus. Those sperm are about all I get out of the experience.

The result, as I'm sure you've figured out by this time, is a fine baby who arrives 283 days later—just about the same amount of time it takes human females to produce their young. Since I'm a dairy cow, I'm allowed to nurse my baby only about three days. After that, I'm supposed to get started on the four tons of milk I'm expected to produce each year to help my owner pay his bills.

What I have to go through to help him pay those bills is not that great, but the one neat thing about my sex life is the total lack of responsibility required of me. Motherhood for a cow may seem frivolous, but at least I don't suffer from guilt attacks because I can't say "No." My biological computer gets all the blame. I just do what comes naturally. That takes away any sticky moral problems and gives my sex life the added bonus of helping my human get some money back on his investment.

 ## Cows Don't Understand Responsibility

Well said, Millicent. Now we can understand a bit more clearly that in matters of sex you simply are not responsible. You're a little like us humans in some ways—you eat and digest your food pretty much like we do, and your heart, lungs, and kidneys work the same way as ours. But you're different in a lot of important ways. Non-humans like you don't understand about moral responsibility or making decisions in their own best interest.

Cattle, for example, are here only to provide those four tons of milk, or maybe be turned into juicy porterhouse and prime rib steaks (or hamburgers if they fail to meet their dairy quota). Whether called "instinct" or "computerized programming," the motivation and drives of the animal kingdom leave no room for scruples. But it doesn't work that way with people. The uniquely human biological computer is but one important difference between people and dogs or cows.

## What Makes People Different?

As a human, made in the image of God, you have been equipped with a special type of intelligence, plus a conscience and a sense of responsibility. You are to be guided and limited by God-given moral laws. Since you are blessed with the capacity for self-respect and personal integrity, you have aspirations about where your life is going in the years ahead. You probably already know that none of us lives in isolation and that the decisions you make and the actions you take sooner or later affect the lives of a lot of other people.

Sure, you have biological urges, too, which may initially surface through an automatic process similiar to those of dogs, cows, and other four-legged animals. But you also have been blessed with intellectual and spiritual facilities for sorting out those urges, evaluating them, putting them in the right category, and keeping them under control. That makes you *very* different from other animals.

Remember, you have parents, friends, and other loved ones to advise you. There are books you can read and a pastor, priest, rabbi, or guidance counselor who will help you if you ask. You can think things through, consider the consequences, and separate the wise from the foolish—and, yes, the good from the bad.

And when you make mistakes—because everyone does—you should exercise your good sense to profit from those goofs. You can take a good long look at your attitude and plan a bit more wisely next time for those wonderful and exciting years ahead.

# 3

## What Does God Have to Do With Sex?

God has a big universe to run and he never makes mistakes in the process. Staying on top of a big responsibility like that must be a twenty-four-hours-a-day-seven-days-a-week job for God. We would guess that it requires a lot of attention just to manage the physics, mechanics, and logistics of the mind-boggling creation he is responsible for.

Our planet alone is inhabited by five billion people, and nobody really knows whether or not there is life similar to ours in billions of other solar systems out there somewhere in space. So, when you consider the magnitude and complications of running the universe, you may wonder if God could possibly be concerned about the way mere humans handle something so personal and so prosaic as their sexual activities.

31

Any teenager, while attempting to absorb the challenging and sometimes confusing elements of life on Planet Earth, has a right to inquire, "What does God have to do with sex?" A young friend of mine candidly expressed his feelings on that score: "Is God any more interested in what I do with my sex organs than what I do with my appendix or my belly button?"

Let's probe that question a little further by asking if it makes sense that God should be concerned at all about our morals. If each person is only one five-billionth of all the human life on an earth where millions die every day (only to be replaced by millions more who are born daily), what difference does an individual's sexual activities make to God?

 ## Sex Was God's Idea

One approach to finding an answer is to remember that sex was God's idea in the first place. Of course, the human sexual apparatus is not patented, but if it were it would be God who holds the patent. Since nobody knows quite as well as the Inventor-Creator how that apparatus is supposed to work, it seems to make sense that we follow his operating instructions.

Don't be surprised that there's a heavenly interest in the earthy topic of sex. God's interest in our sex life computes better if we understand that he loves us—*really* loves us. Loving us perfectly, he wants us to experience as much happiness in life as possible, and that includes proper use of that sexual apparatus he designed, perfected, and caused to function properly.

God's involvement in the matter makes sex intrinsically a clean word, not a dirty one, as some misguided

people imply. The way people create babies is a process carefully and thoughtfully worked out in a divine plan. The formula was not decided upon by a conclave of long-faced theologians or a committee of scrubbed-up obstetricians. God did it all, and my guess is that he had plenty of alternatives to choose from.

 ## A Perfect Plan

Suppose you were asked to design a system for human reproduction. What sort of original idea would you devise?

Your way might be to have women lay eggs like hens, and to provide men with the instinct to crow and flap their arms like roosters when their children emerge from huge eggshells. Brooding the egg, however, might prove an inconvenience for a busy, modern-day homemaker. To avoid that problem, a method could be devised to hatch the egg under a quilt in the corner of the sun porch or the Florida room, taking advantage of the sunlight to generate the required warmth. But that's a crazy plan, of course!

No matter how brilliant our ideas might be, the search for an improved reproductive mechanism would be academic and pointless. The matter has been settled already by the highest medical and scientific authority in the universe. God designed, assembled, and still presides over the intricate process that involves the female's ovaries, egg, and menstrual cycle; the male's penis, testicles, and sperm; the mechanism of sexual excitement; the act of copulation, or intercourse; fertilization and implantation in the womb; the placenta, developing fetus, and gestation period, and the journey through the birth canal that brings a new life into a world. Incidentally, that world contains many other mysteries we don't fully understand either.

 ## More than Biology

There is much more involved in human reproduction than just a biological process. It should be obvious that— through his love and concern for every dimension of our lives—God has made the joining of male and female parts something more than just a way to preserve the human species. He made physical intimacy a source of mystical delight and gratification. However, those pleasures are legitimate only if the intercourse is performed the way God intended it to be done: between the right partners and under the right conditions.

It ought to sober us to realize that the enjoyable aspects of sexual intercourse might have been overlooked or ignored by God when he put the system together. Since copulation is basically a biological function (part of the reproductive process), it could have been tied in with scientific procedures done in hospitals or biology labs. Or sex might have been made a nuisance and necessary evil you could compare with a trip to the dentist, the shoe store, or the barber shop.

The point is that God was under no obligation to make the reproduction process enjoyable. Some of it is not, in fact. For example, childbearing is not the most pleasant experience in the world, though most women describe it as "mystical" and "awesome." So why should *conceiving* a baby be painless? Why not make sexual intercourse as uncomfortable as, say, getting a polio shot or donating a pint of blood to the Red Cross?

Instead, our wise and loving God formed our bodies in such a way that proper use of the equipment he has provided to create new life also makes possible enjoyment that can be the most satisfying, intense, personal, and intimate experience two people ever share.

More than that, God programmed into all his creatures a sexual desire that ensures the propagation of each species. Please note, though, that sex is not a survival need, like our need for food, water, air, or shelter. Anyone who considers sex one of life's necessities is playing against a stacked deck. As strong as the sex drive is, it is subject to conditions and human control.

All this takes humans far beyond the clinical make-a-baby aspect of sex. The caring and sharing of a sexual relationship, when consummated God's way and under God's conditions, provides rewards beyond mere reproduction of the species. Those rewards are bonuses—God's special gift to us as objects of his love—and are available when we follow the Designer's directions. For humans, sexual expression provides physical and emotional fulfillment, whether or not the purpose includes having a baby. But, for reasons only God clearly understands, sexual union is meant only for emotionally mature people with an exclusive lifelong commitment and loyalty to each other. This kind of bonding is found in a marriage relationship (see 1 Cor. 6:18 and Eph. 5:3). That generalization is not determined by clinical studies or popular vote. It is based on a set of values that comes from God.

##  Recreation plus Procreation

It seems plain that God did indeed design sex for recreation as well as for procreation, though the importance of either aspect varies among married couples. The catch is, sexuality functions properly only under the requisites of maturity that the Creator has prescribed, and that is why this book asks a lot of questions about those conditions.

Surely you already know that sex is much more than "birds and bees." That is why a purely biological approach is never good enough in sex education. Biology makes the procreative act as scientific and boring as pollen drifting from stamen to pistil in the plant world. If you take that line of thought a little further, sex could seem as impersonal as having a haircut.

God gave sexual intercourse a deep-down satisfaction that applies whether or not a man and a woman are producing a baby. He also provided stern and specific guidelines as to when and with whom that ecstasy is to be experienced. Ignoring those guidelines destroys the delicate balance of the whole beautiful process and can make sex a frustrating and destructive experience.

Yes, sex is awesome and can be very pleasurable, but it can also be a tricky and dangerous game. The potential benefits are there, but they are often elusive. The finest privileges life offers bring great harm or unhappiness if we use them unwisely.

Getting messed up in the way you handle your sexuality—using it other than in the way God intended—can result in damaging and disillusioning consequences for yourself and others. We'll be taking a closer look at those consequences in some of the chapters that follow, so read on. Irresponsible sex can ruin lives. Don't let it ruin yours.

Now do you see what God has to do with sex?

# 4

## Don't Blame the Toilet Seat

One of the reasons sex is sometimes considered a dirty word is the fact that certain unpleasant diseases involving our sex organs can be passed between partners during sexual intercourse. These diseases are called "venereal," as a questionable tribute to Venus, the Roman goddess of love.

Is syphilis, gonorrhea, or herpes a *love* disease? The idea may have a certain romantic ring, but I can assure you that if you catch one of those diseases, you won't see anything appealing or pretty in your discomfort, embarrassment, and fear.

### Herpes and the Counter-Revolution

Before Acquired Immune Deficiency Syndrome (AIDS) demanded the primary attention of America's scientific resources and the media, Herpes Simplex II was the most talked-about disease of the genitals. Some sociologists credited it with sparking the Seventies counter-revolution against the do-whatever-is-fun philosophy of the Sixties. Herpes is still around, though, and we'll take a closer look at it and two other major venereal diseases here. Then, in the chapter that follows, we will separate fact from fiction where AIDS is concerned—a merciless killer and commonly transmitted through sexual intercourse.

Once upon a time, our civilization recognized that chastity was desirable for moral and religious reasons. That idea took a beating two decades ago, and some adolescents began to take their "right" to sexual activity for granted, even at the junior-high level. When the Pill came along, traditionally accepted ideas about moral values were scoffed at by those who insisted that each person had a right to "do his own thing." Happily, for a lot of smart reasons, young people today are taking a closer look at chastity and adopting it as a personal commitment that makes sense.

Though the highly publicized AIDS epidemic probably holds more terror than most sexually transmitted diseases because it is nearly 100 percent fatal, it has not yet claimed as many victims as Herpes (and the others mentioned above). People are not likely to die from Herpes Simplex II, but some of its victims may wish they were dead. About one out of every twelve Americans suffers today from genital herpes. Nearly half a million contract the disease each year, almost

exclusively through sexual contact. Disturbing statistics like that were changing people's minds about sexual permissiveness even before the AIDS virus was identified and the body count began.

### Tiberius Tried to Stop It

Herpes itself is nothing new. Early in the first century, the Roman emperor Tiberius forbade kissing in public—apparently because a lot of Roman citizens were suffering from a disease they figured was passed along through such romantic intimacy. It is a reasonable guess that the disease was herpes, which gets its name from a Greek word meaning "to creep."

The Pill ushered in the sexual revolution of the Sixties, and about that time medical researchers discovered that there are two types of herpes viruses. One (HSV-1) prefers the tissues of lips of the mouth; another (HSV-2) prefers the tissues of the sex organs. One problem is, those viruses don't wear identification badges.

Herpes Simplex Virus-2 may not be fatal and sometimes its symptoms may be alleviated, but it is considered incurable. Until (if?) researchers find a cure, "forewarned is forearmed," as the old saying goes. Herpes could ruin your life or at least cause your cherished dreams of lasting romantic love to go unfulfilled.

### It Begins with Itching

The first symptom of genital herpes is an itching sensation, usually followed by blisters on or near the penis or vagina that may not go away for three weeks. During this active stage of the virus, the victim may also suffer severe headaches and run a fever. It is during the active stage, too, that herpes is most easily passed along to someone else through sexual contact, or, less frequently, through kissing.

After the active stage has run its course, the virus becomes dormant and the symptoms may disappear, sometimes for weeks or months. Often the victim then *mistakenly* assumes the danger is past. With HSV-2, the symptoms may come and go, but the disease itself will stick with its victims forever—at least until medical science comes up with a cure, if it ever does.

 ## Syphilis Can Kill

Syphilis is a loathsome and dangerous disease, but with the right medicine it can be cured if treated in time. It is a disease more serious than herpes, however, because it can move through the entire body without noticeable symptoms. And, yes, it can be fatal. About 25,000 Americans contract syphilis each year, and in spite of effective and available cures, about 300 victims will die from the disease.

One of the subtleties about syphilis is its low-key approach. A person can be infected for years by the slender, corkscrew-shaped spirochete that causes it and experience no symptoms at all—until it's too late to cure it. A pregnant woman with syphilis may be unaware she has the disease, yet pass it on to her unborn child. This can result in miscarriage, stillbirth, or permanent physical defects the child will have to endure (such as an abnormally high forehead, a flat nose, or peg-shaped teeth).

### Three Stages

Syphilis usually goes through three stages, getting more life-threatening and more difficult to cure as it progresses. Three to six weeks after contracting the disease, the infected person will probably find a small lesion—called a chancre—on or near the penis or the vagina. That is stage one, and at that point a few daily shots of penicillin would probably cure it handily. The chancre usually disappears in two weeks.

About six weeks after the chancre dries up, a rash appears. This may spread to other parts of the body or cause small ulcers in the mouth that are irritating but relatively painless. Other symptoms, such as fever, headaches, and swollen lymph nodes, may appear. Deceptively, this second stage also appears to "clear up," usually after two or three months.

After the first two stages, the victim may have no outward symptoms of syphilis for years—up to twenty-five or even more. During this period the disease is latent, but the spirochete is still there in the victim's body, doing its destructive work. The spiral-shaped microbes are busily spreading through the bloodstream, causing irreversible damage to certain internal organs, including the nervous and the cardiovascular systems.

When a person infected by syphilis enters the third stage, it is probably too late to help him (or her). Infections in the heart and major blood vessels usually prove fatal. Before death, syphilitic degeneration of the spinal nerves causes a progressive failure of muscular coordination known as *locomotor ataxia*. The symptoms are similar to those of spastic paralysis or muscular dystrophy. Inflammation of the brain during the final stages of syphilis can cause gross personality changes and gen-

eral paralysis before the patient's inevitable and un-
lovely death.

England's King Henry the Eighth purportedly died
of syphilis (at the age of 56) after a regal life of noto-
rious sexual indulgence. If he had this disease, there's
no telling how many women he infected in the process
and how many men subsequently caught the insidious
disease from them.

### *Penicillin Can Do the Trick*

On the brighter side, remember that a few daily in-
jections of penicillin usually cure syphilis *if* the disease
is caught in its early stage. That's a scary "if," because
syphilis wastes no time in harming the body's tissues,
and those scars can be permanent. Damage to the brain
and/or blood vessels will likely persist, even after penicillin kills the germs that caused it. Simple blood tests
known as Wassermann or Kahn are available through
public health departments, and these quickly determine
whether or not a person has contracted syphilis. To protect public well-being, most such centers will also treat
the disease and contact a patient's sexual partners for
diagnosis and treatment, if necessary.

 ## Gonorrhea Fights Back

Gonorrhea came to be considered a relatively un-
threatening venereal disease after World War II, when
penicillin had proved effective against the bacteria that
caused it. In recent years, though, the gonococcus mi-
crobe has begun to fight back. Strains of gonorrhea that
resist penicillin have developed spontaneously. Of the

one million cases of the disease reported in the United States each year, about fifty thousand apparently can *not* be cured by penicillin.

Needing another weapon, biochemists developed a more expensive antibiotic called spectinomycin, which worked fine for a few years. In late 1982, however, the National Center for Disease Control in Atlanta announced that gonorrhea strains were showing up that could not be controlled by either penicillin or spectinomycin. Even more expensive antibiotics must be developed as weapons against these stubborn gonococci. For that we can blame the people who still reject the idea that chastity is the best protection against venereal disease.

Gonorrhea affects the mucous membrane of the sex organs and of the eyes, sometimes destroying the vision of babies born to infected mothers. Since the germ is widespread and sometimes undetected, obstetricians apply a few drops of silver nitrate solution to the eyes of all newborn babies to prevent the possibility of blindness caused by gonococci.

For some reason, gonorrhea produces less obvious symptoms in women than in men, in whom it is characterized by a progressively heavier discharge of pus from the penis. If the disease is untreated, it can cause sterility in either male or female.

 ## Abstinence Protects Best

Crude individuals might win a few laughs if they joke about catching herpes, syphilis, or gonorrhea from a toilet seat. But it won't be at all funny if they ever find themselves adding up the miseries that go with it.

The truth is, a toilet seat is not a likely vehicle for spreading venereal disease, since germs left there cannot live more than a few hours at most. Damp towels are more dangerous. Some bacteria can live in that environment for a couple of days or more.

Condoms ("rubbers") and certain germicides offer somewhat shaky protection against transmitting germs during sexual intercourse, but the only sure way to avoid infection is to avoid casual sexual contact. Perhaps the growing threat of sexually transmitted diseases will make more of us rethink the basic principles of chastity in obedience to God's guidelines. Sexual restraint is not only a workable option but has long been recognized as a moral keystone of our society.

When a guy and gal with loving commitment to each other come to their marriage bed free of past sexual indiscretions (and possible disease) and committed to marital truthfulness and loyalty, there will be no fear of disease to ruin their sex life or destroy their mutual respect. As long as they find sexual fulfillment in each other alone, both their consciences and their bodies will remain clean. That's the way God meant it to be when he designed that joyous and intimate union of a man and a woman that comes under the heading of "sexual love."

# 5

# AIDS: A Terrifying Killer

Let's get one thing straight before we go further in considering the gruesome death sentence implied in a diagnosis of Acquired Immune Deficiency Syndrome. Whereas no cure for AIDS now exists—and it may be years, if ever, before medical science can produce one—the chief cause of the rapid and devastating spread of this disease is readily identifiable, scientifically proven, widely known, and easily avoided.

## "Perverted and Promiscuous Sex"

"AIDS has been able to sweep across this nation primarily through perverted and promiscuous sex." A respected congressman from California made that statement on a network TV talk show and was promptly booed by a dozen or more young men in the studio audience. The same young men cheered the comments of an admitted prostitute on the panel who complained that "women of the street" feel libeled by allegations that they are involved in the spread of this frightening disease. The same guys then applauded the panel's homosexual (from the Greek word *homo,* meaning "same") when he loudly protested enforced testing for AIDS because "it isolates gays and other advocates of kinky sex" and unfairly exposes them to public contempt.

Get the picture? The young men booed the congressman, who presented the medically proven facts and offered what seemed a sensible solution. They cheered and supported the homosexual and the prostitute— probably the nation's chief practitioners of "perverted and promiscuous" sex!

The fact that they booed the congressman tells us that some people likely don't want the medically proven facts. They don't want moralizing either. What they do want is additional millions spent on finding a cure, so they can have their cake and eat it, too. Since they don't want their fun spoiled by worrying about consequences, they demand new formulas for "safe sex." That way, their perversions and promiscuity will not be threatened by either practicality or moral values.

Be honest now: If you had been in that studio audience, would you have booed the congressman, too?

 ## A Mysterious Killer

AIDS is not actually a disease that kills directly, like diptheria or meningitis. It is a mysterious virus that attacks our innate ability to fight off invading bacteria and viruses, which constantly seek to make their homes in our bodies and feed on our tissues. The victim is killed not by AIDS itself but by some other disease— perhaps pneumonia—that the body ordinarily could have fought off with the assistance of modern-day medicines. If the immune system that one's body uses to fight microscopic invaders has been weakened by AIDS, invading bacteria or viruses are able to destroy the infected person in spite of medicines that are usually effective.

The simple truth is, the only *safe* sex is sex that is practiced within God's guidelines. When a person has sexual intercourse, he or she is exposed not to just that particular partner but to everyone else that person has ever had sex with, for years past. Since no AIDS preventive is foolproof, the only people virtually beyond the reach of AIDS today are (1) married people who are loyal and faithful (monogamous) to each other and (2) unmarried people who practice chastity. Also at risk are those who fool around with intravenous drugs or receive a blood transfusion from an untested source.

 ## Is Research the Answer?

Should researchers continue to seek a cure for AIDS? Certainly—just as they must continue in the fields of cancer, heart disease, muscular dystrophy, and other human afflictions. But each individual bears a responsibility in the battle against AIDS. Similarly, people who smoke heavily in spite of all the warnings have no right to fault society or medicine because more should be spent on lung cancer research. Can smokers complain because a "safe smoke" has not been found? If they want to reduce their risk of getting the disease, the sensible solution is to give up smoking and remove the chief cause of the threat that can kill them.

Should we also spend millions to educate people about the dangers of doing drugs? Of course, because there are still a lot of youngsters not completely aware of the deadly risk they are taking—and not just because of AIDS. But can a drug addict complain because science has failed to produce a "safe fix"? His best chance for a healthy and productive life is to get his head straightened out and give up the drugs. And if he is smart, he will regard as a valued friend anyone who offers him that advice and tries to help him follow it.

 ## Stopping the AIDS Epidemic

AIDS could probably be stopped in its tracks even now if perverted and promiscuous sex were eliminated across the length and breadth of our nation. That won't happen, of course, but maybe this book can keep *you* from becoming one of those morbid statistics.

The term *perverted* includes what male homosexuals do when they use the partner's mouth or rectum for what a woman's vagina was designed to do. Such sexual practices apparently facilitate the communicability of the AIDS virus. That is why, when AIDS first appeared on the American scene, it was almost exclusively found among males who got their sexual satisfaction with other men—and we'll look at some scary biblical warnings about that in a later chapter on homosexuality. The unnatural expression of their sexual appetites created circumstances in which the killer virus found its way quite easily from one victim to the next.

"Promiscuous" refers to people who recognize no values that would limit their sexual activities to a single partner. For example, when AIDS began to appear among heterosexuals (those who engage in male-female sexual relations), it soon became apparent that prostitutes are among the chief carriers of the disease. It is assumed that they acquire the virus from bisexual men (guys, sometimes referred to as "switch hitters," who have sex with women as well as with men) and pass it along to their heterosexual customers. Remember, though, that "promiscuity" is not confined to prostitutes and their clients!

On the coattails of AIDS has come a new frankness about sexual activity. Today, condoms are openly discussed by kids who not too long ago would whisper little jokes about "rubbers" without knowing for sure what big guys did with them. You probably know that a condom is a thin, elongated rubber "balloon" that fits over the erect penis and is supposed to do the double duty of catching the sperm (thus it is referred to as a contraceptive—"against conception") and also preventing the spread of disease between the partners. A condom is not 100 percent effective, however, in either case. The rubber can come off during the maneuvers of sexual intercourse. Or a defect in the thin latex can produce a tear. A condom is better than no protection, but it certainly does not guarantee "safe sex."

AIDS is rampant wherever people are promiscuous or perverted. Premarital chastity and fidelity between marital partners are among the best preventives. As a young believer whose entire adult life lies ahead, your present choices regarding chastity, monogamy, and sexual preference may well determine not only the quality of the life you will enjoy, but also how long you will live to enjoy it!

DATING IN THE **AID**-IES

# 6

## The Girl Becomes a Woman

There is one special aspect of femininity many women say they would be glad to do without: *menstruation*. Some even call it "the curse"—a term from the Genesis account of Adam and Eve's disobedience and the penalty God imposed upon the woman.

Menstruation is the periodic bleeding following the monthly peak in a woman's childbearing cycle and thus is one stage of the reproductive process. That is why it is referred to as a "monthly" or a "period." (The Greek word for "moon" is *mene* and the Latin word for "monthly" is *menstruus,* so it is not difficult to figure out where the English word *menstruate* comes from.) Some call menstruation "vaginal bleeding," but the blood actually comes from the uterus. Gravity brings it down the birth canal and out through the only available body opening, the vagina.

 ## The Biological Timetable

Menstruation takes place because a female's reproductive system operates on a biological timetable that is part of a master plan. The process that results in monthly bleeding is called "ovarian rhythm," and the twenty-eight–day (more or less) menstrual cycle first starts happening without much warning, usually when a girl is about twelve or thirteen years old. It is not an automatic linked-to-age happening, like getting a driver's license, registering to vote, or "being confirmed" in church, but it usually comes around those ages. However, it can be just as "normal" to begin menstrual bleeding as early as nine years or as late as sixteen.

The menstrual cycle does not continue for a lifetime. Ovulation eventually becomes irregular and finally ceases at *menopause,* for most women somewhere between the ages of forty and fifty-five. That, too, is a more-or-less statistic. Although women have been known to bear children in their sixties, that is quite unusual. Menopause means that childbearing days are over. Except if it results in other physical or emotional changes, most women are not unhappy about entering menopause. The menstrual cycle is an important part of a woman's personal experience for something like half of her "threescore years and ten."

 ## It Begins at Puberty

Let's take a closer look at the way it all starts.

At the onset of a girl's puberty (when the menstrual

cycle begins), several changes take place in her body. Pubic hair begins to grow in her pelvic area, her breasts begin to develop, and her hips become fuller. One day, in the natural course of events, she will need her wider pelvis to bring babies into the world and her mammary glands to feed them. God's plan is making her ready to bear and nurture her children.

Biological chemicals called *hormones* cause all this to happen. You would need a graduate degree in endocrinology to understand everything hormones do, but think of them as microscopic messengers dispatched by various glands and moving through the bloodstream to regulate the body's functions. Researchers have identified at least a hundred different hormones, and there are probably more. Each hormone contains a "key" that fits a "lock" in its target cell, so it can do its work selectively. But right now we are talking about a special hormone produced by an adult woman's ovaries. Called "estrogen," this hormone controls her menstrual cycle and prepares her body to host the fetus when pregnancy occurs.

When a girl reaches puberty, her ovaries begin to release mature egg cells, usually at the rate of one each month. As an egg leaves the ovary and travels down the oviduct, the uterus prepares itself to host a fertilized cell. *Uterus,* as you are probably aware, is the medical term; *womb* is the more widely recognized word. Either term refers to the internal "pouch" where the unborn child is protected and developed until he or she is ready to enter the outside world.

 ## The Egg Arrives

By the time a fertilized egg reaches the uterus, the lining of the womb is thickened and filled with an extra

supply of blood. Its tiny swollen blood vessels provide a nurturing environment for the fertilized egg, which takes hold of the walls of the uterus and grows into a *fetus* (developing, unborn child). On rare occasions, two or more mature eggs travel from ovary to uterus at the same time. If each is fertilized by separate sperm, they become separate embryos, not necessarily of the same sex. When such babies (about 66 percent of twins) are born they usually resemble each other no more closely than do ordinary brothers and sisters. These are called *fraternal* twins, triplets, or whatever. On rarer occasions, a fertilized egg divides into two different parts (embryos) early in its development. When that happens, the twins are the same sex and identical in almost every way, including blood group. You guessed it—they are *identical* twins. It is not exactly a statistic you will want to memorize, but one birth in 87 is a twin birth, triplets are 87 times rarer than twins, and quadruplets are 87 times rarer than triplets. Except for women taking fertility drugs, the odds against quintuplet births become astronomical.

 ## Taking Care of the Fetus

When fertilization takes place, the mother's entire reproductive system automatically ceases its ovulation process and concentrates on the welfare of the *embryo* (the term usually used until three months after conception). Ovulation and menstrual bleeding normally cease during the nine months of gestation before the child is born. To "miss a period" is therefore one of the first hints of pregnancy, though it is not always an accurate sign. Pregnancy test kits, available in drugstores, provide an early and more reliable diagnosis.

Although ovulation takes place around 420 times during an average woman's lifetime, few—sometimes none—of those eggs end up being fertilized. If a male spermatozoon does not locate the egg and penetrate its outer lining within forty-eight hours after it is released from the ovary, the egg dies and begins to disintegrate.

When that happens, the enlarged blood vessels in the lining of the uterus shed their extra supply of blood and return to their normal state until the next cycle begins. As these blood cells are released, the lining "bleeds" and the blood flows downward and out through the vagina. To protect her clothing and to spare herself embarrassment and inconvenience, a woman wears a sanitary napkin outside the vaginal opening or inserts an absorbent tampon into the canal. Now and then a hormonal imbalance or some other physical factors complicate matters and the bleeding becomes excessive. That seldom results in anything life-threatening, but it is wise to consult a gynecologist (a specialist in female medicine) promptly when bleeding is profuse (or unusually scant), or causes debilitating pain, or continues longer than a week.

Menstruating can be a disconcerting experience, especially the first time it happens. A girl's first period seldom chooses a convenient time to start. The bleeding might begin at school, at a party, during a shopping spree, at Sunday school or during an athletic event. If she does not understand that menstruation is a perfectly normal process, a girl may be both embarrassed and frightened at its initial occurrence.

## Adjusting to Premenstrual Syndrome (PMS)

The maturing woman soon becomes accustomed to the inconvenience of menstruation. She usually learns to adjust to the physical symptoms and mood changes that may signal the approach of another period. Those changes vary widely, depending mainly on the body chemistry and physiological functions of the individual. Irritability, depression, or tension may develop a few days before the period begins; some women notice a lack of motivation. One lady complained, "I can tell when my period is about to happen because I'm always hungry. I'll eat anything in sight, especially if it's sweet or salty!" Small wonder, then, that bloating is also a common complaint during the few days before menstruation occurs.

Since there is apparently a physiological basis for the water retention experienced by many premenstrual women, discipline in eating habits pays off—especially avoiding fats, sweets, salty snacks, and other junk foods. One physician adds to this advice: "Drink lots of water and get plenty of rest." If you find yourself in a monthly blue funk or feeling lazier than usual, ask your family and friends to be patient with you and do your best to cope. If the problems seem unreasonably severe, tell your gynecologist about the symptoms.*

Other physical symptoms may accompany menstruation—before, during, and immediately after. A woman's

*PMS: What It Is and What You Can Do About It by Sharon M. Sneed, Ph.D., and Joe S. McIlhaney, M.D. (Grand Rapids: Baker, 1988) combines good advice and real help for PMS sufferers.

nipples may become more sensitive to touch, for example. Some women experience physical weakness, perhaps from the blood loss. Such symptoms usually are considered normal. With a little understanding and emotional support from family and friends, the experience becomes routine for most women.

 ## A Sign of Growing Up

Though some details of this feminine experience may sound grim to a teenager, stay cool. Beginning to menstruate is one of the most important milestones in a woman's life. It is a sure sign that a girl is growing up. Her body is being prepared, through the intricate and miraculous processes God has built into it, for that day when she can bear children and enter the exciting and fulfilling double role of wife and mother.

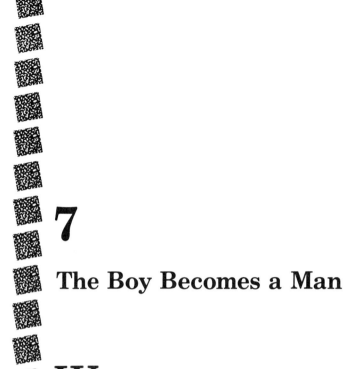

# 7

# The Boy Becomes a Man

When boys grow up, they do a lot more than grow out of their clothes. The transformation from boy to man—as from girl to woman—is called "puberty," and it involves drastic physiological and emotional changes. Some are felt on the inside; others are seen on the outside.

##  A Matter of Hormones

Hair is one of the visible changes. When male puberty starts, hair begins to grow where it didn't grow before: on the face, under the armpits, and in the pelvic area. A boy's legs get longer, his shoulders broader, and his penis and testicles bigger. He begins to experience inner feelings and longings never felt before, and sometimes these frighten and confuse him. It is difficult for an adolescent to understand exactly how he is supposed to handle the new feelings and still keep God's laws and his self-respect, as well as live up to everyone else's expectations.

Those feelings—and the resulting conflicts—arise because of the visible and invisible changes taking place in the male body. Puberty can begin for a boy when he is thirteen years old, though it may not happen until he is fifteen or even older. At puberty, the testicles begin to produce and store up spermatazoa—those microscopic tadpole-like creatures capable of penetrating the surface of the egg that a female produces, thus beginning the process of reproduction.

A lemon-sized muscular gland called the prostate, wrapped around the male urethra just below the bladder, begins to produce seminal fluid. This milky, sticky liquid carries the sperm and protects the lively little polliwogs from temperature changes and other dangers they may encounter on their journey toward the egg.

Sperm are not the only things produced in the testicles. Just as an adolescent girl's ovaries secrete hormones into her bloodstream to initiate her body changes and subsequently govern her ovarian rhythm, so a boy's testes secrete a male hormone. Called testosterone, this hormone sets in motion the processes that cause not only the boy's physical changes but also the shift of interest that characterizes a healthy male who at long last has reached puberty.

 ## Surprise!

One sure sign of adolescence usually takes a teenage boy by complete surprise: the nocturnal emission, or

"wet dream." This curious and potentially embarrasing happening takes place during sleep and usually at night, but it has been known to occur during a nap on the couch in broad daylight. The nocturnal emission may be associated with a dream about girls in general or about an imaginary sexual encounter, but it can also happen without any awareness or memory of the event. Though he is fast asleep, the boy's penis becomes firm and erect, just as it would in sexual intercourse.

This erection can happen simply because a distended bladder or a buildup of seminal fluid stimulates certain nerves, causing an increased flow of blood into the sponge-like erectile tissues of the penis. Nocturnal emissions are evidence of the normal functioning of the intricate nerve-glandular-muscular interaction that makes *orgasm* possible (that climactic moment for male or female when "the whole earth seems to move") and male *ejaculation* (the pumping out of the male's seminal fluid that launches the sperm on its journey into the woman's body). A "wet dream" is the body's way of discharging the oversupply of seminal fluid produced by its newly activated glands. Even though a boy may be sound asleep and have no recollection of the experience, he has a *climax* ("goes off") and deposits his seminal fluid on his pajamas or the bed sheet. He may wake up afterward, hoping he will not have to explain this evidence of his newly emerging manhood!

There is no doubt now that the adult world, with all its responsibilities, lies straight ahead. The nocturnal emission will happen again, and there is no way to predict when or where. The cause is buried deep in a young man's unconscious mind and body, which are stimulated by those male hormones. It is not unusual, by the way, for "wet dreams" to continue well beyond the teen years.

## Suddenly Girls Are Females

Along with adolescence comes a sexual awareness the boy had not experienced before. Those hormones are working hard! Girls begin to attract not only a young man's general interest but also his intense curiosity. He notices things about female bodies he rarely noticed before, or at least never felt were important. He begins to entertain pleasant fantasies based on what he would like to do if he could find a willing partner, assuming he could be sure how to go about it. Of course, he would also have to overcome his fears and uncertainties and keep the whole thing secret from certain people—probably including God.

An adolescent male has occasional impulses to touch—to experiment—but usually realizes that is not acceptable social or moral behavior. Though he doesn't understand how all those mixed emotions can be resolved, he wishes he could find out. He is pretty sure that what he is experiencing is a desire for sexual satisfaction and wonders how to surmount the sizable barriers standing in the way of satisfying that urge.

 ## It's Always There

There is no timetable for all this—no established cycle, as there is in many non-human animals. An adolescent boy's sexual interest is always there beneath the surface, waiting for some form of stimulus to bring it out into the open. Since we live in a culture where sexuality is exploited and pornography abounds—and since hormones are also doing their thing in girls (to complicate matters)—that stimulus is never hard to find. Often a teenager finds himself under heavy peer pressure to throw values and restraint to the winds and get his kicks here and now.

The desire for sexual satisfaction is both natural and normal. However, in a civilized society and particularly within a Christian commitment, this urge can create a formidable problem. A boy's preoccupation with females and with his own sex organs and feelings soon comes into conflict with social restraints and moral standards. It threatens the value system he has learned from his parents, from the Bible, and/or from others responsible for his religious and moral instruction. The feelings emerging from unknown places deep inside him are often at war with a young man's sense of virtue, commitment, and responsibility.

Does that sound like anyone you know? If you recognize yourself in the preceding section, you have arrived at the stage in life when some of your most significant and enduring decisions must be made. You may not realize the awesome importance of your choices—indeed, you may not even be aware you are making such decisions. Just the same, you are beginning right now to form your answer to a crucial question that runs something like this: "What will my lifelong attitude be toward attractive, desirable people of the opposite sex?"

 **Wrong Answers
Impose Penalties**

Ask yourself whether or not you will regard females as fellow human beings, people as entitled as you are to their individuality, their personal worth, their self-respect, their hopes, and their fears. Or will you think of them as sex objects, perhaps provided by some benevolent but amoral creative force to satisfy your own selfish desires? Do you need to be told that the first attitude is the correct one?

Thousands give the wrong answer to questions involving their sexuality, not only imposing penalties on innocent parties, but also paying a heavy price themselves, perhaps for the rest of their lives. Those negative consequences can come in the form of loathsome disease, wasted friendships, sleepless nights, personal neuroses, and ruined marriages. Once a boy has adopted the macho male role of sexual aggressor—constantly bird-dogging for willing females—it is next to impossible for him to regain the sense of dignity and respect that treats sex as a sacred gift that demands one's solemn responsibility.

On the other hand, when a young man makes the right choices and seeks a clear and accurate understanding of his God-given role in sexual relationships, he will find the benefits concrete, real, rewarding, and enduring. He is well on the way to a maturity that will make sex a never-ceasing miracle, with a user's manual that comes straight from God. This involves a choice between what is shallow, cheap, and temporary on the one hand, and what is profound, priceless, and eternal on the other.

# 8

# Creating Harmony

Y ou wouldn't get much enjoyment out of music if it weren't for something music makers call "harmony." If you are not a musician, you probably don't pay much attention to harmony. You would quickly notice something wrong, though, if the right harmony wasn't there. Now I'm going to explain to you how sex is like that.

 **When Harmony Is Missing**

Musical harmony involves the relationship of one note on the scale to other notes above or below it. We must put together at least two notes to have harmony, or create a chord. But there are right ways and wrong ways to combine notes. Some fit together in ways that sound good; others do not. That is because of something technical that has to do with the vibrations of different pitches and the way the frequencies match when they pass through our middle and inner ears and into the brain. When we hear discords, we may not know *why* the notes don't sound right, but something tells us the harmony is missing.

Out of that instinct, laws of harmony have taken shape. Composers know those laws and put them to use, especially when they write musical arrangements and accompaniments. If they didn't obey those laws of harmony, their music might attract attention for a short while because of its uniqueness, but it wouldn't be likely to endure.

The fact is, composers work long and hard to put musical notes in proper relationship with each other, though they have to contend with more than just the laws of harmony. Notes thrown at random into the air are not going to land on the music sheet in the form of a symphony or a great love song—not in a million years. Music that lasts and has meaning to anyone but its composer involves tone, melody, rhythm, intervals, pacing, and other things even more subtle. Somebody has to work very hard to achieve all that.

Music has power. It can leap over social barriers, alter moods in humans and animals, make people fantasize and change behavioral patterns. But whether "music" refers to the military cadence of a marching band, the stirring swell of a symphony, the simple melody of a folk tune, the strident repetition of rock, or the majestic notes of a great hymn, the kind of music people remember gets that way because somebody took the time and made the effort to put it together "by the rules."

## Discord Is Easy

So, anybody can make discord, but it takes skillful hands to make harmony. Sex is like that, too. It has the potential for harmony, but it also can create discord. Only an investment of time, energy, and caring can produce sexual harmony, though the reward and satisfaction makes all that effort worthwhile.

Keeping sex meaningful and harmonious requires more patience and understanding than many people want to give it. The opposite of that often seems easier. To make sex discordant—empty, disillusioning, and plagued by guilt—all you need do is treat it like a piano keyboard that you pound with both hands, ignoring the notes on the music score in front of you.

On the discord side . . . well, everyone knows, for example, that there are women who sell sex. Whether you call them whores, prostitutes, hookers, harlots (the Old Testament term), strumpets, bimbos, or call girls, the job description is the same: they charge men money to be their partner in discordant sex. And *both* buyer and seller are violating the rules of sexual harmony.

It might have hit the movie theaters before your time, but *The Best Little Whorehouse in Texas* made a lot of money for Burt Reynolds, Dolly Parton, and its producers because it glamorized a fictitious place where gorgeous girls were rented out to male customers like lawnmowers from a rental shop. But—glamor or no glamor—is that the kind of place we would expect to find sexual harmony? Fat chance! The idea is to pay your money and take your turn. Then hope you don't catch anything, and be careful no one sees you on your way out. An experience like that makes sex a cacophony or, at best, a dirty word.

Or picture a guy and a gal in a car parked at a lonely spot. The adults who love them and care about their lasting happiness don't know what they're up to. The gal is mostly afraid, and the guy probably is, too, but his mind is on scoring. The pace gets faster and the breathing heavier, and soon they are touching each other in what seem daring places. Then they are fumbling through the motions of peeling off some of their clothes, while one of them may protest feebly, "Don't tear that or Mother will want to know what happened."

The interiors of automobiles, of course, are not designed for that kind of gymnastics. The girl may fight back a little, at least enough to prove she's not "easy." But they finally manage—however awkwardly—to get together. Before she (or either of them) knows what's happened, it's all over. He's finished, and that's it. Perhaps this is his first score, or perhaps it's just another conquest—one more notch in his gun. But what a blow to her self-respect—and to his, if you really think about it!

This is "sex," but not the kind that creates any harmony. You make no memorable music that way. Besides, you can't hear the symphony when you're frightened out of your teeth and afraid of every shadow or rustling breeze. We're talking about discord here.

Let's face it, though: throughout the history of mankind sex has been a popular pastime, and not all of it has taken place in circumstances sanctioned by marriage or enhanced by love and genuine caring. For countless people in our own society, "sex" means what goes on in secret and in dark places, with the constant fear of being discovered. These people use their sexuality in activities that involve lying, cheating and stealing, all rolled into one ugly bundle. There is no harmony in that kind of sex; it is discordant with a capital D.

 ## Making Beautiful Music

We can be grateful there is a happier picture. Think of a home where husband and wife consider sex as an intimate and beautiful sharing of their love and commitment, a rapturous experience so precious that they waited happily for each other. Likely they have found as much pleasure in making love as in any other privilege they share. So they continue to guard the experience and strengthen it through loyalty, truthfulness, and faithfulness to each other.

But a couple cannot develop that kind of relationship overnight. As their love for each other grows, it gives them the patience and determination to work out problems and develop the harmony that can add such pleasure to their lives. It is through trial and error together that a man and woman learn what could be learned no other way. They must explore together, with smiles and sometimes laughter, the full meaning of sexual interaction between a man and woman who share a special commitment of love. Then they discover through their shared experience that harmony, fidelity, and trust work beautifully to solidify their union.

Is sex a discord for such a couple—something to be hidden? Far from it! Oh, sure, they may lock the bedroom door so their kids can't barge in on them without knocking. But that's not because they are ashamed or afraid. That's because sexual intercourse is the most personal and intimate joy a married couple can share together. It was never intended as a spectator sport and should be enjoyed only in complete privacy.

When you think about sex, think also about harmony. That's when sex remains clean and wholesome. If you keep it that way, I promise you will avoid a lot of the discord that is taking the real fun out of life for millions of people.

# 9

## Procreation or Recreation?

Sex education does not involve just turning out biological experts who are learned in the way certain body parts function and in the science of human reproduction. It also means—and certainly with special limitations—understanding the mysteries of sex as a means of human joy. The scientific aspects of sexual expression are all about *procreation*. Just as properly, the second category can be thought of as *recreation*.

Is there someone reading these words who feels the idea of "recreation" ought not to be included in a sex-education book for young teens? Let me offer my sincere apology for unintended offense, but I am asking you to trust me and read on.

It is not surprising that biology courses usually bypass the fact that humans find sex pleasurable, because what biology is all about is science. But appreciation and joy are among the realities of sex, too, and these enhancements are produced by love, understanding, and commitment. God apparently had dual purposes in mind when he designed human sexuality. The most obvious purpose is no doubt procreation, since that is what ensures the continuation of the human species. But no less significant to the healthy adult is the second purpose treated in this chapter: recreation.

 ## Recreation, Not Sport

Please don't be misled by the term *recreation*. What we are considering here is not a fun-and-games attitude toward sexuality. We are not talking about the kind of cheap frivolity that reduces the idea of sexual intercourse to the level of a leapfrog contest or a wrestling match on a gymnasium pad. No, we are discussing here one of God's special gifts to human beings that make us superior to all other creatures in this world.

For humans, sex is not just a reproductive instinct or a biological chore. God made sexual expression a very special experience for us. He included in the prescribed use of human sexuality an intimate feeling of oneness, a total sharing for two people who truly love each other. Under the "right" circumstances, there is a satisfaction that is unique, which is why a sex-education book should provide far more than technical data about the human reproductive system and its processes. To make the picture accurate and complete—to educate responsibly— we need to speak of the pleasure and satisfaction available to those who treat sex in the way God intended.

## Doing It God's Way

The reason for this chapter is simple and logical. If young people don't learn in the proper way and from the right source about "sex as recreation," some of them will enroll in informal self-education seminars (the kind conducted on beach blankets). All too often, that kind of research backfires and causes the participants grief and regret—the very opposite of the pleasure they are seeking.

You must know and understand the truths, the promises, and especially the warnings that apply to recreational sex. Since your need to know about that is as urgent as knowing the mechanics of how babies are made, we're going to tackle that assignment right now.

At the top of that special warning list about sex as recreation is a fact already emphasized: sex works best when God's instructions are faithfully observed. Does that sound like a grumpy grown-up who is constantly trying to keep kids from having fun? I'll tell you honestly that my aim in writing this book is to reduce the risk that you will sacrifice long-term happiness on the altar of immediate gratification. Plenty of sadder-but-wiser guys and gals who have done it their own way—not God's—have learned a painful lesson in that regard. If they could reach you now with a message (and if they could persuade you to listen) they would urge you to "be patient." That is a #1 rule, since "proper" sex is worth waiting for.

 ## Understanding the Unconscious

You may be unaware of this, but behind our conscious thoughts is a huge collection of unconscious impres-

sions. This unconscious part of our personhood constantly sends up information that provides direction for our lives. The way we respond to beamed-up-from-the-unconscious data contributes a great deal to either our happiness or our misery.

Many of those unconscious impressions, whether healthy or not, were imprinted by our childhood experiences. They include attitudes, facts, and ideas we picked up from parents, playmates, schoolteachers, Sunday-school lessons, and a lot of other sources. But what about "impressions" of less-certain origin—like, for instance, the way salmon know in which river to lay their eggs and how migrating birds know which way is south? Are similar drives rooted in human personalities? Instead of the mental compasses and maps like those used by birds and fish, consider the possibility that God placed a system of moral values in our memory core—a system we sometimes choose to ignore. Do you see a resemblance there between our ignoring God's values and a salmon's trying to swim up the wrong river? How about robins on an icy winter day heading by mistake toward the North Pole?

 ## Ignoring God's Guidelines

Everybody knows we *can* ignore moral guidelines if we choose. But not everyone is yet aware that we cannot avoid the confusion, restlessness, and frustration usually resulting when we take matters into our own hands and try to eliminate proven truths.

Sure, sex can seem daring, intriguing, exciting, exhilarating, and adventuresome, even when (or perhaps *especially* when) it ignores God's guidelines and rebels against biblical values. But that kind of "fun" falls short of the overall pleasure and fulfillment God programmed into sex for humans who follow his directions. We discover truly lasting sexual joys only when physical intimacy includes a commitment of love and respect by both parties. Then there is a special climate of loyalty and mutual concern that makes sex an experience to be cherished, not a venture in lust to be regretted later.

Deceit, anxiety, and guilt have the power to block or diminish the marvelous recreational purposes God built into human sexuality. Those negative feelings can change potential beauty and pleasure into ugliness and fear.

 ## Mending Fences

Let me give you a real-life illustration of how past experiences can affect one's present sexuality. A lady came to me for counseling because her husband was being chummy with another woman in a way the wife resented. He flatly denied he was being unfaithful, and I believed him, but his wife remained indignant about the situation.

When I questioned the couple routinely about the quality of their sex life, I got a noncommittal shrug from the husband and no response at all from the wife— at least not at first. Finally, however, when I pressed her for an answer, she blurted out, "Well, if you must know, it's about as enjoyable as making a blood donation!" This woman obviously thought of sex as neither beautiful nor gratifying nor something shared by two people in love. It didn't take long to get from that outburst to the admission that they had both given up on romance long ago. Neither could remember when last they had sex together.

Only gradually did the whole truth come out. Finally the wife was able to talk privately about certain harrowing sexual experiences she had had in the eighth and ninth grades. An older boy in her neighborhood had talked her into "having a little fun," and their fumbling efforts to have sex had gone on for two years. Eventually they had been caught. The resulting guilt and shame—along with some memorably severe punishment—had adversely affected her view of sex from that unhappy moment on.

Can you see that this woman and her husband were paying the price for her indiscretions of long ago? The wife's coldness became understandable in the light of her adolescent experiences. And her husband's flirting and indifference—though certainly not excusable—were fueled by her disinterest in sex. He had no way of knowing the real problem; his wife had not told him. Her sexual mistakes in junior high had robbed them both of a whole lot of happiness and very nearly destroyed their marriage.

That story has a happy ending. After a lengthy and painful process, both husband and wife reaffirmed their desire to continue sharing their lives. In due time, she overcame the emotional handicap that had been blocking her sexual pleasure. Now the couple is finding happiness in a relationship no longer haunted by the ghosts of a destructive youthful sexual experience.

 ## Collecting Proper Memories

You are packing stuff into your own memory core right now, aren't you? Is it raw material that will properly influence your thoughts and feelings in days to come and relationships yet to develop? Your experiences of today, tomorrow, and next week may turn up years later to handicap or even enslave you. You can make your own rules for recreational sex if you insist, but you'll also have to live with the consequences down the road. Avoid like smallpox any experiences that might threaten the most precious of all relationships yet to come: your marriage.

# 10

## The Phantom Father

**M**arine biologists at the New York Aquarium were left shaking their heads and flapping their tongues over a forty-pound but full-grown female octopus with a tentacle radial measurement of nearly ten feet. Nobody knew she was pregnant, but one day she gave birth to more than a thousand half-inch–long babies.

It was not the miniature size or the number of babies that stumped the scientists. The problem was identifying Papa Octopus—or, more specifically, explaining his total lack of identity. The aquarium people swore that no male octopus had been near the mother during the critical time period. They had captured the mystifying lady eight months before in Puget Sound and had then flown her across the continent to New York in a saltwater tank. She had been alone in the aquarium ever since, with no contact at all with gentlemen octopi (octopuses?) who could be held responsible for her condition.

It is well known to marine biologists that *gestation* (the process of producing a fully formed baby, from conception to birth) takes only three months for an octopus. This particular female had been nowhere near a male octopus for at least eight months. Yet it is also a scientific fact that mama octopi never get pregnant without the help of prospective papa octopi.

So, the question is, who was the phantom father and how and where did fertilization take place?

 ## Theories Vary

"I'd have to assume the tank's filter system was responsible," one aquarium biologist speculated. "We do have male octopi in some of the other tanks, so I guess their sperm somehow passed through the connecting pipes, got by the filtering system, and fertilized the female's eggs." (Neat explanation, huh?)

"Impossible!" sneered another biologist. "The male octopus uses a special tentacle for fertilizing the female's eggs. Free-floating sperm couldn't do that in a million years!"

"Okay, so what's *your* theory?" asked the first scientist.

"Well, maybe the mother octopus actually mated months before, while she still lived in the ocean, and some unknown circumstances managed to delay fertilization until three months ago," the second replied. He shrugged then and added, "Yeah, well, I know it sounds improbable, but has anyone got a better idea?"

Other marine scientists merely frowned, scratched

their heads, and headed for the library to probe more deeply into their biological reference books.

 ## An Unsolved Puzzle

Care to make a guess about the phantom papa? Well, the only creature who might have all the facts is the mother octopus, and at last report she was stonewalling it. So far, she has maintained a dignified air of silent innocence—surrounded as she is by myriads of wiggly half-inch octopi. It looks as if the little guys are doomed never to know who Daddy is.

This is a mystery not likely to be solved. Birth of octopi in captivity under *any* circumstances is rare—very rare. The above-mentioned New York Aquarium caper was only the second captive octopus litter (brood, maybe?) on record.

Was the filter system responsible? Was it an incredibly rare case of delayed fertilization? Was it some mysterious alchemy of the briny deep that forever will confound the scientific world—as does the Bermuda Triangle? Right now, your theory is as good as anyone's. Meanwhile, please pardon the smug look on the mug of Mama Octopus.

 ## No Phantom Dads
## for Humans

Never try to tell such a paternity story about yourself! No one will buy it. If you get pregnant, or if you make someone pregnant, you cannot claim the amazing malfunction of a filter system or some sort of freak

biological happening. When an unmarried girl turns up pregnant, the ugly story is usually soon public property. It is seldom difficult to identify the daddy.

Neither is it hard to reconstruct the events that led to the embarrassment. Some guy took the girl where she shouldn't have gone and did to her what he shouldn't have done—and she shouldn't have let him do it. The guy may still be bragging in the locker room about his sexual conquest. But even if he keeps quiet, she is usually the loser, left wondering why something like this happened to her. There's an innocent victim to consider, too: the baby. What sort of life lies ahead for this innocent kid?—assuming that someone doesn't decide to resolve the problem by killing the unborn baby before he has a chance to find out.

 ## Time for the Shotgun?

Maybe the prospective grandpa should get out the old 12-gauge shotgun and make the creep marry his daughter. But what kind of solution is that? The chances are she would be facing a lifetime of misery, handcuffed to a man she neither loves nor respects. He would enter a loveless marriage too, resenting his new wife because "she let it happen."

That story line is not fantasy. In real life, pregnancies that are unexpected, unwanted, and humiliating happen every day. There are ways to guarantee that you'll never be among the cast of characters. But if you *should* find yourself caught up in a drama like that, don't try to kid anybody with that dumb octopus story about a phantom father. If you are a girl facing such a pregnancy, the only thing that resembled the octopus in your particular experience was probably the guy's hands. They were so busy you thought he had eight of them!

If you turn up as such a victim, there'll be no mystery. Everyone will know what happened and *you* will know who did it: the fast talker who insisted there was nothing to worry about. He was the one who whispered into your ear so romantically, so enchantingly, "Something that feels so good can't be wrong."

Well, by that time you'll know better.

##  Are Contraceptives the Answer?

Maybe the guy is right, in a way. There may be "nothing to worry about" as far as *he* is concerned. With you, though, the story is different; you can worry plenty. If you went along with that tired old bromide about romance and good feelings, you have no one to blame but yourself. As an unmarried mother, you'll have plenty of worries for a long time to come.

Would using a contraceptive have made things different? After all, married people have means of preventing conception, and one way or another those are available to unmarried people as well. Sure, for girls who decide to reject the Bible's value system, there is always the Pill to take care of the possibility of pregnancy. But the Pill is nothing but a chemical that keeps a woman from ovulating. Like any other chemicals introduced into one's body, it can have unpleasant side effects. It can even be life-threatening. That's why the Pill is legally available only through a physician's prescription. By the way, many married women who try the Pill find they cannot tolerate it.

You are probably aware that other contraceptive devices and procedures besides the Pill are available. Sure, most of them can reduce the chances of unwanted pregnancy, if that is all the user is interested in. But you need to be aware, also, that there is a bunch of possible complications. IUDs (intrauterine devices) were installed semipermanently in years past by physicians to prevent pregnancy. But the devices caused so many medical problems and generated so many lawsuits against manufacturers and doctors that they have virtually disappeared from the market. Removable diaphragms that block the entrance to the uterus can be fitted by physicians, but many users find them uncomfortable. Now and then the devices cause infection.

Isn't there an easier way? Well, drugstores carry a choice of vaginal jellies, creams, spermicides, suppositories and foams, and all of these contain chemicals that stop the sperm *if all goes well in the process.*

 ## There Is Also Disease

Contraception does not always go well, and the margin for error with all of the methods mentioned above is risky. The possibility of unwanted pregnancy is always there. And what about disease?

For male use, there is the much-publicized condom. But the condom's protection factor is far from 100 percent for the prevention of either disease or pregnancy. All of these facts are the practical part of the reason that God's way calls for chastity among unmarried people.

I discussed this chapter with gynecologists, who added another warning note. They all said that the girl, not the boy, stands the greater chance of coming up a loser. Sexual activity not only poses for her the risk of pregnancy but also increases the likelihood of contracting pelvic inflammatory disease or other common infections peculiar to a female's sexual organs. Such diseases, the doctors tell me, can result in tissue scarring and possibly in eventual sterilization or malignancy. A sexually active unmarried woman is considerably more likely to develop cancer of the cervix than those who have followed God's instructions. Since the cervix is the little neck at the lower end of the uterus, guys don't even have one to worry about!

The fact is, short of chastity, the only sure way to avoid pregnancy involves surgery, but even that does not stop the transmitting of disease. For the man, a vasectomy can sever the tiny tubes by which spermatozoa travel from his testes to be mixed with his seminal fluid. For the woman, another kind of surgical tube-tying prevents eggs from reaching her uterus. The problem with both procedures, though, is the time, expense, and discomfort involved, plus the fact that the surgery is often irreversible. It can eliminate for a lifetime the possibility of having children.

 ## The Practical—and Moral— Solution

The sensible solution, then, is abstinence. I think we could reach that conclusion totally apart from morals, conscience, or religious principles. It is just as possible (and wise) to "say no to sex" as it is to "say no to drugs." The practical, down-to-earth, and fail-safe approach to the entire subject of both unwanted pregnancy and debilitating venereal disease is still the one the Lord has been offering us so patiently all along. Our Creator really does love you. That's why he is pleading with you not to indulge your sexual urges until the right time and right person come along. You can afford to wait until marriage. In fact, you can't afford not to!

# 11

## Finding a Teammate

mazing, isn't it, the amount of information programmed into a silicon computer chip? Well, the lowly watermelon seed also contains an impressive amount of data. More mind-boggling than that, (with a microscope) look inside a small fish egg in a mass of salmon roe if you really want to talk about programs!

### The Watermelon Miracle

It is said that experts can spit watermelon seeds for championship distances, though it's not yet an Olympics event. Important as it may be to some people, potential spitting distance is not part of the seed's DNA code. Watermelon seeds have hidden talents more astonishing than the possibility of being spit thirty-seven feet.

Toss one into good sandy soil and add fertilizer, a few weeks of sunshine, and enough rain, and it will multiply its weight 200,000 times—maybe more. Those pesky little watermelon seeds are programmed to multiply and rearrange their molecules at a fantastic rate, but don't plant them if you want turnips. Nothing changes their program. Watermelon seeds only produce melons with striped green skins over white rinds that encircle luscious red cores.

In that red core are hundreds of seeds just like the one you planted. All are okay to spit, if necessary, but each is programmed, or designed to perform the same growth miracle. You could repeat the process next spring if a sandy field in the right climate were available— and the next and the next, as well. Nobody knows exactly how that happens, but nobody has to. Maybe God just designed things that way so you and I, in season, can slurp up watermelons and spit the seeds for ever-greater distances.

 ## Back to the Beginning

The basic story is not much different with certain fish roe. You will find another of those incredible reproductive processes in the biography of a large game-fish known as the Atlantic salmon. This tasty guy with the distinctive pink flesh lives in the salty ocean, but not all the time. To make sure the species survives, each *Salmo salar* returns every year in the fall to the freshwater stream in which it was hatched. That's right—out of all the millions of freshwater streams emptying into the Atlantic Ocean, the salmon somehow "remembers" which one, and also knows what time of

year to go there. Every salmon swims back to the place its life began. Fish that reproduce that way are called anadromous.

First the salmon navigates unerringly to the right stream, no matter how far away it is. Then the fish swims leisurely upstream (*against* the current) at a rate of three to four miles each day. If it must clear obstacles or get beyond waterfalls, it can leap as high as twelve feet out of the water.

In October or November, each female salmon lays about 20,000 eggs, depositing them in a depression in the stream's bottom, carefully excavated by her tail. The male salmon's job is to fertilize the eggs by spreading millions of his sperm over them. Both fish have then done what they are programmed to do, so they head downstream and make their way back to the ocean. Soon they are swimming and feeding happily in saltwater until it is time to make the spawning trip again the following season. For reasons known only to the Master Designer, it doesn't work that way with Pacific salmon (sometimes called Chinook). That species spawns once and then promptly dies. For the hapless Chinook, this adds to the whole procedure a decidedly somber note.

 ## Right on Schedule

Several weeks after the salmon eggs are fertilized, they begin to hatch. Then those freshwater streams are filled with millions of baby salmon, eagerly searching for insects and other succulent tidbits so they can grow up and become a new generation of salmon. And those almost unbelievable behavioral patterns are programmed back into them, and into their children, and their children's children, and so on.

For two years, these little salmon kids develop in fresh water. Then the new generation, grown-up now, finds its way downstream and back to the Atlantic Ocean, although those clever salmon never forget the exact stream in which they were hatched. When fall rolls around again, they join other salmon in the same reproductive ritual in the same stream—provided, of course, they haven't ended up at your neighborhood fish market or in a can on your grocer's shelf. Since they were not originally programmed in how to avoid the commercial fisherman's net, 300 million pounds of salmon meet that fate every year.

No one has ever explained that homing instinct. Since Mom and Dad Salmon didn't stick around, we know that the little guys weren't taught navigation by their parents. Obviously we're seeing God's mystical silicon chip, programmed exclusively for that particular species of fish.

##  So What?

There is a reason, of course for all that background material about seeds, salmon, and silicon chips. It's to focus our attention on the human infant, who is something else entirely. That little baby is an especially helpless creature, yet one with really complicated responses and needs. A lot of those infantile responses and needs are found *only* in humans.

Watermelon seedlings and young salmon, for example, don't need to be loved—but human babies do. Baby watermelon and salmon don't need to learn to talk, read, or do the multiplication table. Little people must be taught, trained, and shown how to do certain things. For that, they must study, learn, and observe the behavior of other humans. They need models to show them how things are done, what the consequences are if they are done the wrong way, and how much better it is when they are done the right way.

Unlike Mom and Dad Salmon, human parents are accountable for the care and nurture of their babies. They bear a heavy responsibility for seeing those little bodies, minds, personalities, temperaments, characters, and spirits properly developed for the experience called "life."

 ## We Need Help

A tiny baby left to care for himself—unlike young fish or watermelon seeds—would die. Even if, through very unusual circumstances, a young child managed to survive on his own, he would likely turn out an emotional, ethical, and social misfit. Little humans are dependent upon big humans to provide what they need to grow "in wisdom and stature and in favor with God and men" (see Luke 2:52). Deprived of that opportunity, they have been known to end up in big trouble.

Parents must see to it that their child's physical, mental, social, and spiritual capacities are developed according to healthy patterns. You know from experience how easily kids can pick up the values and priorities someone else shows or teaches them. Young people deprived somehow of proper parental modeling should never use that lack as an excuse for all their bad choices, but they certainly are handed a handicap. If parents are not persistent and persuasive in their guidance, or if they make little sense, kids end up uncertain as to what values are true and real. Even when a child is fortunate enough to have two loving parents, the patience, wisdom, and commitment of both must be consistent. Parents, then, are a partnership—a small "team" collaborating toward a common goal.

##  Following Higher Directions

God provides a blueprint for parenting, and things always go better when his guidelines are followed. Naturally, the human blueprint is different from the one in watermelon seeds. And we don't resemble that salmon with its mysterious instinct to return to its birthplace for spawning. In other words, a lot of what we humans need to know is not inborn, but must be taught to us.

As humans, we require guidance, instruction, discipline, and nurture. Two people who make a baby bear the responsibility for meeting that baby's needs. Everything needed for that is included in the package we grown-ups are handed, right along with the human ability to reproduce our species sexually. "Making a baby" is only a small part of the whole story. The heavy *responsibility* of parenting goes hand-in-hand with the *privilege* of sexual reproduction. Every life that is brought into the world requires a vital child-parent relationship if it is to develop into a healthy and happy human being.

The Bible says a lot about parenting. It also gives believers an encouraging promise in Proverbs 22:6: "Train a child in the way he should go, and when he is old he will not turn from it." Love, faith, patience, prayer, instruction, persistence, and good examples are all part of God's program to develop a child into a responsible, believing adult. In the Bible, you can find memorable illustrations of both successful and unsuccessful parents. In 2 Timothy 1:5, for example, the apostle Paul pays tribute to the mother and grandmother of his best-known protégé. Although these two women were not blessed with believing marital teammates, they somehow raised Timothy to be a fruitful servant of Christ. God's Word also tells us about the weak parental methods of Eli, the wimpish high priest (2 Sam. 2:12–25). His disciplining of two rebellious sons was apparently limited to a wrist-slapping "Why do you behave this way?"

As already mentioned, one way to define a marriage is to say it represents the formation of a partnership—a team with a purpose. The team has an especially awesome assignment when it achieves parenthood. Then it must provide meaning, direction and nurture for the lives resulting from the union of their bodies. That is a purpose that goes far beyond the scope of watermelon seeds and fish roe.

 ## Forming the Team

When boys and girls arrive at their teen years, at least to some degree they begin choosing up sides—yes, forming two-member teams with someone of the opposite sex. Choices made during teen years have much to do with whether or not you end up part of a winning team when you are ready to choose a lifetime teammate. When you look at it that way, you begin to realize how much careful thought—and prayer as well—ought to go into finding that teammate. But *finding* the right person is only part of it. Just as important is the job of *becoming* the kind of person the teammate you choose can love, respect, and desire.

An exciting adventure and a heavy responsibility will begin the moment you and your teammate commit yourselves to each other, but the accountability becomes even more awesome when your team starts producing those helpless little creatures who will call you "Mom and Dad." Make sure that your partnership represents a winning combination and will be working toward a shared goal.

# 12

## The Rules of the Game

 **W**hat could be dumber (or more comic) than a basketball team wearing roller skates? Or try to imagine football players running their plays on bicycles or a bowling match done with tennis balls. Just as self-defeating would be a big-league baseball game where everybody makes his own rules and all the umpires are thrown off the field.

Chaos, right? That's because every game has rules, and the only way people can play and make sense of it is for everyone to know the purpose of the game and play by the rules.

Of course, just knowing the rules is not enough either. Athletes seldom hit their peak until their middle twenties, and for some very good reasons. It takes years to develop strength, speed, coordination, and stamina, just as it takes time to learn the game itself. Professional

sports make terrific demands on players, so they must review the fundamentals of the game until those instincts are deeply imbedded in their minds and bodies. The way to the top is paved with practice, practice, and more practice. The achievers must have sharp eyes, quick reflexes, steady hands, and team spirit. But that's not all. Athletes don't get to the top without something special called discipline.

##  Under Control and Authority

Discipline means putting yourself under external control and authority and following a prescribed pattern of behavior. I like the high-school football player's definition: "Discipline is ignoring what you want to do and doing what you have to do." It's the way to achieve the primary goal—which, in sports, is winning. Determined effort and self-denial are essentials for that. Assuming there is talent, discipline is the key to success on the playing field.

As already mentioned, athletes have to accept the fact that their game is played by the rules. That, too, is a matter of external control and authority. Players seldom get a vote where rules are concerned, since the important ones have been drawn up and imposed on the game by someone else. Referees and umpires have those rules memorized and are there to see they are enforced. That can be tough to do, because the way rules are interpreted sometimes alters the outcome of a game.

Consider the Claytonville Clods, who had the state basketball championship sewed up until the last period in the final game. They had everything it took to win, and everybody considered them the heavy favorites. But their star forward and top scorer was benched for excessive fouling as the final period began, and they suddenly found themselves outclassed. One of the team's few weaknesses was lack of back-up for the key position of forward. But the rules say "five fouls and you're out," so there was no joy that night in Claytonville. The rules hit them hard where it hurt the worst, and the Moetown Marvels walked off with the title.

 ## Notice the No-Nos

The next time you watch an athletic event, listen for the whistle and watch for the no-nos. There are lots of them, and some are more obvious than the rest. Certain restrictions are understood by everyone, right up front. For instance, basketball players may not report for the game wearing football cleats and overcoats. They are not allowed to walk down the court with the ball under an arm or to stick elbows in other players' ribs. There are plenty more rules, of course, and the referees watch like hawks to catch any violations. A player has to stay inside the black line around the court—and if a shot doesn't go through the hoop, no point is earned. Sure, those are "negatives," but take them away and the game would be meaningless.

For obvious reasons, football players are not allowed to kick each other in the stomach, (even in the noseguard position). Tackles may not gouge out each other's eyeballs or break each other's arms, no matter how intense the game. On a less violent level, the quarterback has only thirty seconds to get his team from one play to the next; if he takes longer than that, his side is penalized five yards. If the ball doesn't go through those two slender poles at the end of the field, the place-kick for the point is no good, no matter how loudly the fans protest. There would be disaster on the gridiron without the enforcing of those rules.

 ## Sex Has Rules, Too

Sex is definitely *not* a game, but it does have rules. Sex means a lot of special things—mystery, wonderment, togetherness, and the miracle of producing new life. But it has sensible rules, and a lot of them are no-nos. Believing humans accept the fact that God himself has given sex those negatives for good reasons.

Adultery is a well-known biblical no-no. Adultery refers to violating the sanctity of marriage by having sex with someone other than a marital partner. Fornication is forbidden, too—that means sex without a marriage commitment. God makes those no-nos plain enough in his Word for everyone to understand.

"Do you not know that the wicked will not inherit the kingdom of God?" Paul insists. Then he adds, "Do not be deceived. Neither the sexually immoral nor idolaters nor adulterers nor male prostitutes nor homosexual offenders . . . will inherit the kingdom of God" (1 Cor. 6:9–10). This passage concludes with the urgent advice that believers "flee from sexual immorality" (v. 18).

 ## Be Your Own Referee

Though sex is not a game, it does have referees and umpires with eagle eyes ready to detect every infraction of its rules. To your surprise, you may find the harshest

and most unforgiving of those judges is your own conscience. When the whistle blows, it's often that inner
voice reminding you, "That's a no-no. Watch it. You're
about to step over into foul territory." That's when a
real champion pays strict attention.

We are all blessed with sexuality, but maturity and
responsibility are part of the rules. Succeeding at what
has been called (perhaps inaccurately) "The Game of
Life" demands self-discipline. Becoming a winner means
playing the game under an authority that lies outside
yourself. Sometimes that means ignoring what you *want*
to do in favor of what you *have* to do to confirm those
lasting, God-given values and achieve your personal
goals according to his purpose.

# 13

## Sex with Yourself

"Is anything wrong with masturbation?"

I'll wager you've asked that question—though not necessarily aloud—more than once. The reason for the private conversation is that masturbation is a very personal subject and not easily discussed with other people. Probably the people you are most afraid to discuss it with are the ones most interested in helping: your parents.

It's hard to say, by the way, exactly where the word *masturbate* comes from. But *turbare* is the Latin verb for "agitate," and we don't need help in figuring out that connection. The prefix—*mas*—is more difficult to identify. It might relate somehow to the Latin word *manus,* meaning "hand." Whatever its origin, in English the word means the practice of titillating one's sexual organ with one's hand. And it is kind of embarrassing to talk about it, right?

Why embarrassing? Well, that's about as private as any subject we could think of. The fact is, we are rarely comfortable discussing super-personal things, and that pretty much describes masturbation. We are not likely to talk about it, even with close friends, and the last thing most kids want to do is risk possible humiliation or punishment by discussing the subject with parents. As a result, young people have to make do with whatever information comes their way. And some of that is unreliable, depending on the source. Well, here's information you can consider official.

##  Is It a Perversion?

Let's consider first the "weirdo" question that you may wonder about. One reason people shy away from the subject of masturbation is the fear that fooling around with their own private parts might be a shameful perversion that "normal" people never indulge in. That unfounded notion probably explains the dumb and tasteless jokes people sometimes tell about masturbation—mostly people who seem to suffer from a twisted sense of humor.

The fact remains, though—talk about it or not—that "sex with yourself" does happen to a lot of normal guys and gals. It happens behind locked bedroom doors, usually under the blanket or sheet at night. It also sometimes happens under strange and unexpected circumstances. The result of these occurrences is often a troubled conscience for a teenager. If the resolution not to do it again does not last long, the problem can become worrisome. Who can he or she talk with who is capable of resolving it—of shedding light on such a delicate subject?

So the question remains: "Is anything wrong with masturbation?" Many worried teens find it especially difficult to get an answer that makes sense.

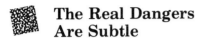 **The Real Dangers Are Subtle**

Let's make a straightforward response right up front: most of the strange notions going around about the fearful consequences of masturbation are ridiculous! You can take my word for it that masturbation doesn't make hair grow in the palm of your hands or cause "water on the brain." It won't lower your IQ, drain your sexual powers, cause paralysis—or make you stoop-shouldered, bow-legged, or bald-headed. No, masturbation never gave anyone acne, ulcers, warts, or flat feet, and never resulted in going blind or even having to wear bifocals. You can set your mind at ease on all those silly notions.

But masturbation *is* capable of causing at least two unhappy consequences. You will want to be aware of those while establishing the priorities and values you will live by as a believer in Jesus Christ.

Basically, for some people, masturbation can turn inward the feelings associated with sex and make it an unnatural "me"-centered experience. Once begun, self-stimulation is a difficult sexual habit to break. Concentrating on that private experience can rob the masturbator, little by little, of the ability to share the experience of sex with the one the Lord will provide as a life partner later on. Many of the problems even Christian couples run into along the hazardous highway of married life—can be linked to sexual incompat-

ibility. This, in turn, is frequently traceable to psychologically disturbing experiences suffered by one or the other partner during earlier years. Obsession with self-stimulation can be one of the barriers to healthy marital intimacy.

 ## Some Complicated Responses

Sex involves psychological responses that are probably more complicated than in most other human experiences. When people consummate their love in sexual union, it is nothing like throwing a baseball, hemming a dress, or spreading butter on a piece of toast, all of which call for mainly physical reactions. Sexual expression involves certain responses of the body and mind that are both physical and voluntary. But much of sex is also involuntary—a part of the mystery of our bodies. The male's erection, the female's lubricating, and the orgasm experienced by both are involuntary, but that implies that sex is psychological as well as physical. Its success and fulfillment (or failure) depend on some things that are conscious, some that are almost conscious, and others we are not conscious of at all. That is the reason it is so important to be concerned about the development of all three of those areas of our mind: the conscious, the subconscious, and the unconscious.

### Not Designed to Be Solo

When we summarize Bible texts about men and women and their sexual activities, it is plain that God intends this special human relationship to be an inti-

mate sharing between two people who are committed
to each other. They are to be permanently joined together as one in his sight and in the eyes of the world,
with special and carefully nurtured loyalties and feelings for each other. For them, sex is something that
continually builds their relationship, not something that
tears it apart. It never frightens, causes concern, or destroys the self-respect of either partner. With all the
sharing that is built into its consummation, sex is definitely not designed to be a sensual bonus that boys and
girls bestow upon themselves while hiding from prying
eyes. Sexual fulfillment is meant to be a duet, not a solo
performance. That seems an especially valid warning,
considering the possibility that obsession with "sex with
yourself" during teen years can threaten the ability to
enjoy it with the right person when the right time and
circumstances arrive.

### Problem Number Two

But that's only one problem, and I suggested earlier
that there are two. The second one may be even more
threatening to long-term happiness than the first.

Even though self-stimulation is done in strict privacy,
it is often linked in the mind of the masturbator with
an imaginary sex partner. That encourages little side
trips into the realm of fantasy that are totally unrelated to reality. Although the imaginary sexual encounters that accompany masturbation often precipitate
disturbing patterns of guilt, there are worse dangers
than that. Our minds can play terrible tricks on us, and
sex is probably the area where acted-out fantasies are
most likely to occur. Encouraged by the sexual conquest
that took place *only* in their imagination, young people

have been known to get carried away and make unwelcome suggestive comments to the girls or boys of their dreams. That's trouble enough, but it's not the worst of it. A few have even resorted to criminally aggressive sexual acts, such as rape or other violent behavior. When that happens, it's goodbye to friendships, reputation, acceptance, and even freedom!

##  Digging a Psychological Rut

Masturbation is at best a futile exercise in fantasy. At worst it can contribute to delinquency and threaten eventual sexual fulfillment. Except in extreme cases, masturbation probably does no physical harm. However, it does encourage the mind to fix itself on sexual goals that otherwise might not be achieved and imagine they have been accomplished. That can spin off serious emotional problems and, in the end, result in serious mental illness.

Masturbation tends to dig its own psychological rut, and the rut can become a dangerously deep one. If you are experiencing a problem—if your worry and guilt mechanisms are working overtime or you are becoming preoccupied with self-stimulation—it's probably time to bite the bullet and talk it over with someone you have reason to believe will understand. Self-stimulation of one's sexual organs may give a moment or two of physical pleasure, but it can lead slowly but surely away from genuine sexual enjoyment when the right opportunity—God's opportunity—finally comes.

# 14

## Gays and Lesbians

A couple of interesting terms going the rounds these days probably confuse some teens. That's why we'll take time in this chapter to review the *facts* about homosexuality—especially the Bible truths involved. You have probably heard people talk about "alternative lifestyles" and "sexual preference"—expressions that often come up when the conversation turns to gays and lesbians. Usually those expressions are used when people set out to defend homosexual behavior.

###  "It's Our Way of Life"

Now and then the citizens of our major metropolitan areas are treated to the sight of hundreds of homosexuals marching through their city to demonstrate for full social acceptance of their unnatural lifestyle. It adds considerably to the confusion that among the chief sponsors of "gay parades" are certain churches classified as Christian, but with membership rolls composed primarily of admitted gays and lesbians. Did I say "admitted"? Perhaps "boasted" would be more appropriate. "It's our way of life and we like it," one marcher recently bragged, "so we're demonstrating to force straight people to accept us as equals." It's a "respectable alternative lifestyle," we are told—just a matter of exercising one's "right" to individual sexual preference.

 ## Perversion Is Spreading

Even without those parades, there is not much doubt that sexual perversion has been on the increase in the United States for some time now. This and a lot of other social ills reflect our national denial of God and rejection of the values he has clearly given us. Perhaps more ominous than that, sexual deviates who once hid themselves in closets of shame are coming boldly into the open. They declare loudly their sexual preferences and even commend their unnatural choices to others.

A national society of homosexuals has been organized for the purpose of promoting social acceptance "for those whose taste in sex happens to be different." This society publishes its own newspaper and has a legislative lobby. It openly expresses contempt for "straight people who assume they are the only ones with rights in the area of sexual expression." The hope of this and other such organizations is to dignify homosexuality and establish it as a normal and legitimate lifestyle.

Gays and lesbians work hard at getting this message across and have already achieved many of their goals. Once upon a time, though, they were referred to in sneering whispers as "queers," "fruits," "fairies," "faggots," "weirdos" and a few other names more explicit and even less complimentary (and hardly appropriate to a book for Christian teens).

 ## The "Gay" Church

There is a rapidly growing national church denomination whose membership is made up primarily of gays ("gay" usually refers to homosexual men) and lesbians (homosexual women). These people profess to be Christians, but they apparently have no problem with biblical warnings against the sin of the sexual perversions they practice. I am referring to God's Word on the subject, not just the opinions of moralists, schoolteachers, evangelists, and even some psychologists. If gays and lesbians considering themselves Christians cannot accept the Bible's authority on the subject of sexual deviation, you wonder how they can claim the truth and promise of John 3:16!

A New York City pastor I know has been approached more than once by a man asking the pastor to marry him to another man. "These men weren't kidding," the pastor told me. "They were dead serious!" In each case one of the pair saw himself in the role of a head-of-the-household husband and the other was to play "submissive wife." They saw nothing unusual in wanting to become Mr. and Mrs.!

This pastor is a committed Christian, a Bible believer,

and a man of principle and integrity. You can be sure
there's been no such wedding—at least not in *his* church!

 **Blind Prejudice?**

Probably not everyone feels an instinctive revulsion
toward the idea of homosexual behavior. What do you
picture two guys doing when they "make love"—or two
gals? How do you react to the idea? Does the mental
picture make you cringe a little?

Some people say it is simply a matter of ignorance
and blind prejudice to disapprove of someone who gets
his or her sexual kicks through intimacies with a person of the same sex. They may even insist that a person's sexual preference is merely a matter of genes—
chance biological happenings beyond human control.
When boys prefer boys, or girls prefer girls, did it "just
happen" that way? Should no one criticize or condemn?
Is there nothing anyone can or should do about it? Some
permissive citizens wonder angrily why society assumes
the right to concern itself with what two people do in
the privacy of their own bedroom. That "privacy," by
the way, is not a real issue, since nowadays homosexuals
seldom attempt to hide their actions.

"Private rooms" and "private tubs" are for rent by the
hour in "adult" movie houses and sex-oriented spas
across the land. Pornographic literature and videos that
cater to the unnatural tastes of homosexuals are freely
circulated in specialized "sex shops." In short, laws have
been changed or enforcement relaxed in order to allow
gays and lesbians the "freedom" they demand. Who is
to say how God figures in all this?

# The Bible Has the Only Answer

In whatever form perverted sex takes place, most of the questions about why it occurs cannot be answered in a few words. Thick books have been written by physicians, psychologists, and sociologists—all theorizing about the causes of homosexuality. Moral implications and social and personal consequences have been thoroughly explored as well. New theories about ways to "cure" homosexuals appear regularly.

Sadly, though, the people who make our laws are yielding more and more to the political pressure of a very loud minority and turning deaf ears to what God says in his Word on this controversial subject. Our nation is slowly changing its attitude and softening laws that for centuries have penalized perverters of sexuality. Society—sometimes supported by "the church"—does its best to quiet the voices of those who warn against homosexuality. The general public is apparently expected to be more permissive and less judgmental than in "puritanical" days. For the Christian young person, however, the important question is not "What does popular opinion say?" or even "How do the writers of sex-education books handle the subject?" The bottom line is "What does the Word of God tell me about homosexuals?" After all, it was God who created our sexuality.

## Lot had a Problem with Gays

The Bible's first reference to defiled sexuality is in Genesis 19. We are told that two angels visited Lot to

warn him that God soon would destroy his wicked adopted city of Sodom. (This was a city given over to hedonism, meaning pleasure seeking in general. Believers know this as not a myth or a legend, but an event in history that really happened nearly four thousand years ago. Sodom had a definite geographical location somewhere near the Dead Sea.) When the Sodomites learned about Lot's visitors, "They called to Lot, 'Where are the men who came to you tonight? Bring them out to us, so that we may have sex with them' " (Gen. 19:5).

That's pretty blatant, but people today can be just as crude and irrational when blinded by lust. Desperate to protect his visitors, Lot offered the Sodomites his two virgin daughters instead (our idea of "hospitality" makes *that* pretty difficult to understand!). The Sodomites who were gathered in the streets knew what they wanted, and they resented Lot's calling their intent "wicked." They practically tore Lot's door off its hinges in a frenzy to satisfy their perverted passions. This really was a city full of weirdos!

### God's Judgment

Shortly after that, God's judgment was poured out on Sodom and on Gomorrah, another wicked city. The perverted citizens at Lot's door were struck blind and the city was wiped off the face of the earth. *Sodomy,* ever since, has been one technical name for unnatural sex, especially as practiced between men.

The apostle Paul, inspired by the Holy Spirit, gives us the Bible's clearest statement about God's attitude toward homosexuals and their depraved practices. You can find that statement in the first chapter of Romans, but it won't convince you unless you accept the fact that this is the Word of God, not just "preacher talk." The following passage really does apply today just as it applied in Paul's day:

"Therefore God gave them over in the sinful desires of their hearts to sexual impurity for the degrading of their bodies with one another," Paul wrote to the Christians in Rome (Rom. 1:24). ". . . God gave them over to shameful lusts" (v. 26a). Was he writing about homosexuals here? Well, let's read on: "Even their women exchanged natural relations for unnatural ones. In the same way the men also abandoned natural relations with women and were inflamed with lust for one another. Men committed indecent acts with other men, and received in themselves the due penalty for their perversion (vv. 26b–27).

Pretty plain, isn't it? That ought to remove all doubt as to what Paul was writing about. The Bible couldn't be more specific without sounding like a pornographic magazine: "Furthermore, since they did not think it worthwhile to retain the knowledge of God, he gave them over to a depraved mind, to do what ought not to be done. . . . Although they know God's righteous decree that those who do such things deserve death, they not only continue to do these very things but also approve of those who practice them (vv. 28, 32).

So, call homosexuals what you will; even dignify them with that "gay" title if it makes anybody feel better. But God says their so-called alternative lifestyle is despicable in his sight—a personal foul in the game of life that carries a fearful penalty: death.

##  Still Perplexed?

There is always a possibility that one of you readers has already begun to experience strange and confusing feelings for someone of your own sex. Maybe you have even gone off the deep end and had a homosexual experience. Is that just the way your genes are arranged, a sort of nothing-can-be-done-about-it nudge in the direction of a life sentence to homosexuality? Do your feelings or that act constitute a permanent defeat that eliminates the possibility of a serious and productive Christian life? Not at all! They are a warning, though, that the time is ripe for serious Bible study and prayer. Lay the problem before the Lord, who not only forgives but also heals and restores. He works through human helpers, so an honest talk with a caring and compassionate parent, pastor, Sunday-school teacher, or counselor can help someone who is struggling with confused sexual feelings. If those are not available, there may be choices among other mature persons with genuine Christian commitment and confidence in the authority of the Word of God.

There are often identifiable reasons for mixed-up feelings about sex. An understanding Christian adult can help young people deal with them. Our doubts and mistakes don't have to ruin us for life. In fact, they provide us with some of our most valuable lessons and growth opportunities. It is true that a huge variety of lifestyles are waiting out there, and we choose from them as the Lord develops our individual character and personality traits. However, for a style to be acceptable to a Christian, it should never include the sexual perversion that the Lord condemns. No one who really gets to know God will settle for the misery that goes with that kind of disobedience. Always remember that homosexuality, according to the Bible, is a sin deserving of death.

The term *faggots,* in days gone by, referred to bundles of sticks placed on a fire. Do faggots still burn? Well—excuse the bad pun—but they surely burned in Sodom. And from what the New Testament tells us, it sounds as if they will burn also on judgment day. Be careful to stay out of scorching distance when the fire from heaven descends!

# 15

## Dating or Mating?

The way some teenagers go about it, you would think there was nothing to attract people of the opposite sex to each other except sex.

I hope I'm not referring to you, but watch that big dude who counts legs and ogles brassiere sizes in the corridors between classes. This guy is not interested in what a girl really is as a person—her intelligence, her personality, her values, her character. His only interest is in her body parts and probably in whether or not she is generous with them. It would never occur to him to judge one of those "chicks" he watches by any standards other than the size and shape of what he would like to get his hands on.

## "What Do You Have in Mind?"

You can find the same dude on the telephone several times a week, talking to his current target about "a date," but what he's really got in mind is not dating. It's *mating*. He's not thinking of things properly described as "social." Whatever the preliminaries, his real plan includes a bit of heavy breathing in a secluded spot where no one will interfere. Then he hopes to add another scalp to his collection of female conquests.

The way he puts the question when he calls rarely gives a hint of his real intentions. He starts out with, "Uh, doing anything Friday night?" That is often all he can think of at the moment to get his secret plan in motion. If the girl knew what really was on his agenda, she would scream before he got in another word, "Not with you, you big oversexed ape. Get lost, octopus!"

But she may not be a very skillful mind reader and has not yet learned to recognize the symptoms. Perhaps she's been hoping to get to know this guy. And what red-blooded American girl, after all, wants to sit at home on Friday night and play Monopoly with her kid brother? So she purrs that by an odd stroke of fate it's the one night that just happens to be open at the moment, thank you. "And what would you have in mind?" she asks him.

In *mind*? Monkey business, of course. But letting her know that little secret would sink his ship before he launched it. What he has in mind is discovering how far he can go when he finds a nice secluded spot. He hopes to give himself something to brag about next week when he and his buddies get together to boast about their weekend conquests, both real and imaginary.

What this turkey really wants is to make connections with any reasonably sexy-looking female who will let him have his way, and he makes all those telephone calls to put the process in motion. Unfortunately, although he's not typical, his target may soon be convinced that she's the only one who really matters to him in all the world. What he has in mind is not *her,* but scoring. What he wants to do is called "making out," and this girl is merely the one he's selected for that privilege this week.

##  A Contest of Wills

If the guy answered her question truthfully, it would ruin everything. So what he mumbles is something like, "I dunno, why don't we take a ride in my old man's car over to Middlesville and see what's on at the movies?"

Movie or no movie, what the evening actually is slated to become is a contest. Working up the necessary courage, Joe parks and tries to see how far he can go. Susie tries to see where she can stop him and still hang on to her virginity—not to speak of her self-respect and her popularity with the boys. She probably says, "Now you just stop that, Joe! Just because I let you kiss me a couple of times, what makes you think I'm *that* kind of girl?" The contest won't be over until one comes out a winner, which makes the other a loser.

Is that dating—or is it mating? When you plan a night on the town with someone of the opposite sex, how would you describe your real purpose? Probably you see your date as a person, but then again, maybe he or she is more like some *thing* to be used for your own selfish purposes. In that case, maybe you'd better just quit while you're ahead. The winner of one skirmish can be a loser over the long haul.

## Make a Choice

The question is, are you willing to settle for the shallow, superficial experience of touch-and-go lovemaking? Why not consider your boy-girl experiences as part of the far more satisfying and exciting discovery of learning who you really are? Learning what makes other people tick—and caring about their feelings and ideas—is a necessary facet of maturity. Dating makes that kind of "education" a pleasant, shared experience.

No intelligent teenager needs a textbook to suggest interesting things guys and gals can do together for fun, and still come away feeling clean, fulfilled, and really glad things stayed that way. Plenty of excitement is out there in the social world to make dating an enjoyable activity without an ounce of sex involved. Probably your church has carefully planned programs for people your age. If not, ask someone why—and try to get a youth group started. Besides the church, there are fun places to go and pleasant things to do, some involving little or no money.

Whenever and wherever they are together, two people who respect each other and want to build each other up can talk about hundreds of topics and ideas that make the whole world come alive with new meaning. You won't have to look far to find wholesome entertainment and challenge—athletics, water sports, games, recreation, hobbies, parties, and rap sessions. Even doing homework together can expand a friendship to dimensions never before imagined. That's right, I said *even homework*!

 ## Using or Building?

When you look at that guy or gal in the classroom or corridor or in the car with you, do you see a whole hu-

man being, someone with a mind and a living soul valuable to God? Is it your right to *use* that person? Or is it your responsibility to help that person build on his or her potential? Well, honestly now, which is it—use or build? You can't do both. And furthermore, do you think it's any of God's business which of those options you choose? If you are a Christian, you know the answer, don't you?

Take a good look and see if you recognize in the other person some important feelings, impressions, opinions, experiences, and insights that can expand your own mind, too, and help you in your search for meaning and fulfillment. If you can recognize those aspects of someone else's personhood and respect them, you are way out in front. You'll be dating, not mating.

But if all you see when you go out on a date are the physical characteristics of the opposite sex—a nice-looking face and body whose secret biological parts happen to complement your own and whose external qualities turn you on—well, you've got a serious problem and it will probably get worse. Maybe you should talk it over with someone you respect, someone who can explain about one-on-one relationships.

If you've got that problem and do nothing about it, you're putting scar tissue on your psyche, and likely on someone else's as well. Those are difficult scars to erase. In the process of inflicting your insensitivity upon another, you may be stealing from both of you a wonderful segment of life and an important ideal no one really can afford to do without.

# 16

## Sex Is a Four-Letter Word

A five-year-old kid had her crayons strewn all over the living room floor, scratching away intently, when her father asked what she was drawing. "It's a picture of God," she replied, going right on with her work.

"Oh? But nobody knows what God looks like," her father informed her.

She paused for a moment, as if in thought. Then, "They will when I get through," she assured him confidently and returned to her drawing.

How do *you* picture God?

No, we haven't suddenly changed the subject, because the way each of us treats our sexuality depends, in a sense, on the way we picture God. What we think about God shapes our attitude toward sex, as in every other area of our behavior.

## Thinking Right About God

Think that over for a minute. I'm saying that people who have a settled, accurate concept of God are less likely to mess up (or mess around!) than people who haven't reached that point. The kids who get themselves in the most humiliating predicaments are usually those who cling to whatever screwball notion of God happens to appeal to them at the moment.

Achieving a right understanding of God starts with a genuine personal commitment to Jesus Christ. That's the beginning of a biblical—and thus accurate—concept of God. After that comes a lifetime of learning and growing, but you can count on its being a better life than it otherwise would have been.

There are right ways and wrong ways to think about God. Do you believe that's really a matter of opinion? Sorry, human opinion doesn't matter here. That vital, personal discovery has made the difference between happiness and misery for millions of people through the centuries. The right way to think about God is the way *he* reveals himself in the Bible. The wrong ways are the thousands of different "religious" ideas *people* dream up, vainly trying to define the way God is and how they think he runs (or ought to run) his world. Some people would follow just about any concept of God as long as he fits the picture of the way they would like reality to be.

 ## God's Four-Letter Word

In chapter 3 we looked at what God has to do with sex. Here let's consider a few misconceptions about who

God is, how he deals with us, and the way all that affects our attitude toward sex.

Even though in English we use only three letters to
spell it, s-e-x is actually a four-letter word. No, not the
four-letter word that might immediately pop into your
mind, but one that comes straight from the heart of
God. This word belongs in a special way to God and to
his children on earth. The very first definition for "sex"
in the divine vocabulary is the four-letter word spelled
l-o-v-e.

If you are confused about God in general, you might
not understand this "sex is love" stuff. Maybe you figure
that our Father in heaven is like a school principal—
and a mean one, at that. Some people think of God
mainly as a killjoy or a spoilsport, a stern judge who is
determined to see we get no fun out of life. For such
people, sex is often viewed as something sneaky, a forbidden pleasure to get by with when God isn't looking.
A lot of others would say that God the Creator, if there
ever was such a being, has nothing to do with the way
we live now.

Other people think of God as a mythical and thus
imaginary figure or would describe him as part of a
pantheistic collection of gods and religions, basically all
the same. How do you feel about that? If those were
accurate views, believers would be delving only in su-
perstition, and what anyone does about sex would be
nobody else's business. If God were not around, sex and
morals would be whatever we want to make them. The
sexual vocabulary wouldn't begin with "love," but with
words descriptive of smut or used for laughs. Our chief
concern would be making sure the wrong people were

not listening when we talked dirty, assuming that we even cared about that!

## 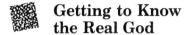 Getting to Know the Real God

But all true believers base their concept of God on something they share, no matter what their denomination or local church affiliation. It's something called "revelation." That's a theological word, but don't let it put you to sleep. Pay attention! It's a way to describe what God *reveals* as truth about himself. God is not whatever people happen to theorize, he is what he tells us and shows us he is. We get to know him only because he reveals himself to us. We learn about him mainly from the Bible—his Word—and through Jesus, "the radiance of God's glory and the exact representation of his being . . ." (Heb. 1:3). The better we know the Bible, the better we understand God.

Biblical revelation is important to each of us. Without it we could never know who God is or the way he works. We would never understand about his love and why he should care about the way we live.

Through the centuries, Christians have been called "people of the Bible." That is because we get to know Jesus in terms of what the Bible teaches. Are you a person of the Bible? If you meddle with the authority of the Bible, you hang huge question marks over Jesus himself. You raise serious doubts about everything he did or said. That kind of doubting questions the truth of Christianity and makes it "just another religion."

To find out who God is, we Christians don't look to church traditions, theological opinions, popular vote, or "religious" theories. We trust what he shows and tells in the Bible. Since the ultimate truth about God comes through biblical revelation, "What does the Bible teach about that?" is the first question we ask when we want to know anything about him.

 ## God's Responsible Love

The first step in understanding God is a truth we have heard thousands of times: "God is love." Love is not always godly, but God is always love. Since he is also a lot of other things, we fit all those qualities together for a complete picture. But understanding God on the subject of sex begins with believing that he really loves us. Like a caring and responsible parent, he demonstrates that love by requiring behavior that *he* knows is best for us, since we seldom know ourselves.

A wealthy yuppie in Jesus' day asked him how to inherit eternal life, and the answer surprised him. We read that "Jesus looked at him and loved him (Mark 10:21). Then Jesus gave his reply, which had to do with obedience. Although it was not what the young man expected, the answer was rooted in Jesus' love.

Here is a special kind of love, a caring and forgiving love that tells us what is true and right, not just what we want to hear. God's love will deliver us from our own foolishness, but only if we trust him. We are lucky he doesn't say, "Do whatever you want; it's no skin off my nose if you mess up." No, God's is a responsible love. If we trust him to do so, he will always give us his best.

 ## Love Without Lust

So we're talking about clean love—love without lust. God's love focuses on *giving,* not on *getting.* This perfect love was at work when "he gave his one and only Son . . ." (John 3:16). God's guidelines about handling our sexuality come from that kind of love. We could guess he isn't surprised when humans complain and protest or kick and scream in rebellion. And he isn't shocked when we goof. In either case, he forgives and goes on loving. But that doesn't change the rules or the guidelines about what is right behavior.

God allows us no excuses and provides no reason to misunderstand the rules. He forbids sex outside of marriage in such crystal-clear passages as "Flee from sexual immorality. All other sins a man commits are outside his body, but he who sins sexually sins against his own body" (1 Cor. 6:18). In due time those sins will catch up with us, even if it doesn't seem that way at the moment of disobedience.

 **Who Really Knows Best?**

The human mind asks, "How can this be bad if it feels so good?" The Word of God says, "It is God's will that you should be sanctified: that you should avoid sexual immorality" (1 Thess. 4:3). The real question is "Who knows best—God or our messed-up human reasoning?"

God's requirements for sex include terms like respect, responsibility, caring, clear conscience, and commitment—words that have their roots in love, not lust. All that shows God's love in action. In his own perfect time and way, he has promised us the desires of our heart—in sex as well as in everything else.

That explains why sex is an incredibly wonderful four-letter word. As believers in Jesus Christ, we must do our best to give it the place God intends. We will find that our ultimate happiness is most secure if we faithfully keep sex safe within the boundaries of his l-o-v-e.

# 17

# The Hedonist's Trap

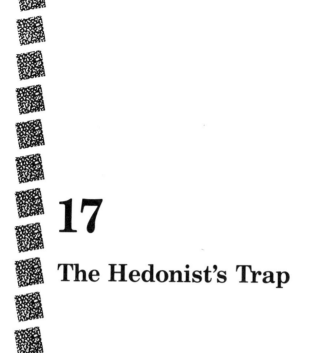

$A$re there 'hedonists' among your friends?" I asked.

"Not me," one junior-high girl responded. "I'm only allowed to go around with Methodists or Presbyterians." Very funny!

Another smart guy sounded off with, "My folks have always been Democrats."

Okay, I'm sure you get the point. But *Hedonism* isn't something you belong to or register as. It's a philosophy of life and it has no membership card. It's a value system—or better yet, an *un*-value system—and it's possible to be a hedonist without knowing it. The word *hedonism* comes from a Greek word meaning "pleasure." It got into our vocabulary because people with that philosophy believe that having fun is what life is all about.

Well, isn't it?

## Keeping Pleasure in Perspective

Don't get me wrong. Having fun has its place, and we're all glad it does. Nobody in his right mind wants to go through life with a long face—never joking, never chuckling, never getting a kick out of life. Think how terrible it would be never to enjoy anything or smile or be thrilled or get excited. Life would hardly seem worth living if we never experienced the pleasures that God provides for every normal human being.

Here's the point: having fun is not the *purpose* of life. That means we must beware of the guy or gal whose personal philosophy is "Live it up. Have a ball." Or "Eat, drink and be merry. Who cares anyway?" Or even, "If you haven't tried it, you're missing something." A lot of pagans wandering around in the jungle knew better than that, and most of them learned their lesson the hard way.

Remember Samson in the Old Testament? He started out in life with a live-it-up philosophy that couldn't tolerate the religious hang-ups of his godly parents (see Judg. 14:3). "I'll have it because I want it!" was his unspoken creed. Sure, Samson believed in God. In fact, he held a position of authority as one of Israel's judges. But he couldn't get rid of the notion that life centers around wine, women, song, and doing things *his* way, not God's. In the end, he went out in a spectacular blaze of glory, but only at an enormous personal price: his life.

 ## Samson Couldn't Say "No"

Though Samson wiped out a lion with his bare hands and wasted a thousand Philistines with the jawbone of a donkey, he couldn't say "no" to a sexy chick from Gaza named Delilah. He was a hedonist who broke the hearts of his parents, betrayed his fellow Israelites, became a slave, had his eyeballs gouged out, and went down to misery and defeat. Because Samson was physically strong but morally weak, the fun didn't last. If you consider all that a religious myth, some kind of made-up object lesson, I've got disturbing news for you. Samson's authorized biography takes up four chapters in the Book of Judges and is confirmed by the Jewish historian Josephus. The account ends with a dramatic final appearance (right in the hometown of the girl who betrayed him) when Samson crashes down Dagon's temple on his own head and kills the evil Philistines as well. Those are facts of history. These sad but real happenings all took place in Palestine along the eastern shore of the Mediterranean Sea, maybe 1,200 years before Jesus was born.

The misguided principle that wrecked Samson's life goes hand-in-hand with the modern idea that restraints are for the birds. Hedonistic philosophy says, "If something is enjoyable and doesn't hurt anybody else, it can't be a problem." People with those empty values may even get pious and say they are motivated by love and devoted to making people happy. Hedonists say it is "immoral" to press our personal standards on someone else and a waste of time to worry about what someone else thinks. "Since sex makes people happy, then let's all have lots of it," they say, implying that there should be no restraints because there are no moral absolutes. But Christians say that we *do* live with absolutes. Just the devastating spread of venereal diseases should make hedonists rethink their philosophy. Instead, their concern is focused on practicality, on how to indulge in "safe

sex." As if the only problem with promiscuous and perverted sex is whether or not people could die from it!

 ## Staying Safe *and* Happy

Actually, the only *safe* sex for unmarried people is sex kept at a respectable distance. A safe society is one with standards and restraints. No absolutes? Try living in a culture that allows people to steal, lie, beat up on each other, or bed down with anyone who suits their fancy. The place would be a moral pigpen, wired to self-destruct before you could say "Playboy."

People are inherently bad, not good. The Bible says that all of us need to be changed. Though Jesus has redeemed us, we have to be taught, motivated, controlled, and restrained as we go along. We need help from beyond ourselves in a lifelong program of learning, growing, and developing according to God's plan.

Having fun is *not* what life is all about. Getting acquainted with God is a better way to describe life's purpose. Life is all about respecting God's standards and living wisely and well, with as few regrets as possible. That is surely a much more workable and rewarding philosophy than hedonism any day in the week. Samson would agree that God's way is not the shortest route to what we call "fun," but it certainly is the surest way to real and lasting happiness.

# 18

# Garbage In, Garbage Out

IGO—meaning "Garbage In, Garbage Out"—is a common expression in our computer age. It means that computers don't have minds of their own: they just cough up what's been loaded into them. If a human operator makes mistakes while programming, the computer tosses back the same mistakes when printout time comes. If the operator complains, someone will probably remind him, "Well—GIGO—What else could you expect?"

## Programming Our Minds

What all of us may not realize is that our minds, like computers, can also be victims of GIGO. The load of garbage collected in human brain cells can get so heavy

151

that some people end up buried under it the rest of their lives. Others just reek with its smell. Chances are, you haven't thought much about that.

Remember the old bromide "You are what you eat"? On that basis, maybe you've decided a lot of people you have to live around have eaten their weight in turkeys the last few years. Well, make room for the idea that we are all also what we *think*. We may not be as much as we think we are, but sooner or later we come to realize that what we think *is* what we are. The way we think is the root motivation for the way we act, and the way we think can be traced to what we program into our minds. That's true whether the programming is conscious or unconscious—deliberate or accidental.

 ## Controlling the Input

It seems likely, then, that if we want to control our output—what we say and do—we have to choose carefully the information we take in. Avoiding burial by the garbage means screening out the stuff that has no place in our mental computers. If GIGO works, then TITO works better. That stands for "Truth In, Truth Out." (Maybe the "T" ought to stand for "Treasure.")

But wait a minute! Perhaps you are wondering how we eliminate the garbage when the world around us is so full of it. People are so loud and brassy with their weird ideas. And aren't we surrounded by temptation? Society's claims and promises are so persistent, and they are often enticing. Even when something deep down inside warns us that it's mostly garbage, the stuff grabs and holds our attention anyway, and it becomes awfully difficult to ignore.

### Sex Sells

You would have to be either blind and deaf or born and raised on another planet not to notice how blatantly sex is used in advertising. Sex is often the theme or emphasis in media ads, regardless of whether or not it has any connection with the touted product. For example, a small ad that has appeared regularly in the *Miami Herald* socks the reader right in the eye with just the word *SEX,* in huge letters. Under that, the copy reads, "Now that we have your attention . . ." and goes on to mention the product (which, of course, is totally unrelated to sex.) Some readers may find it difficult to take very seriously a company that stoops to this kind of advertising nonsense, but the gimmick must pay off. The ad continues to appear in the *Herald,* day after day, year after year.

Sex sells, a fact that is impossible to miss, especially in print media and on television. The question is, how can the human mind be so irrational? For example, what does a sexy girl and a huge cat draped across the hood of an automobile have to do with the quality of the car? Does that somehow make it a smarter buy? For that matter, what does sex have to do with shirts, shoes, refrigerators, or even shampoos and after-shave lotions? Yet, when you take time to figure out the way advertisements in all those categories get the reader's attention, you will often discover sexual overtones, some quite subtle but others very obvious. The advertising constantly thrown our way helps create the load of garbage

some people carry around without realizing it. Sex really sells, but the prospective buyer is better off controlling his input. That way he can know when to buy and when to say "No sale!"

##  That's "Entertainment"?

And about music, TV, movies, and other entertainment media, what can we say that every teenager hasn't heard a thousand times already? Sure, we would have to outdo ostriches in burying our heads in the sand if we tried to avoid *every* reference in the entertainment world to sex and violence. But wouldn't you expect a person—young or old—who professes to love Jesus to make at least an honest effort to be selective? That's particularly important if we take time to remember that we really are what we think.

"It's a new generation, Mom and Dad. Things are different from your day, so what's the harm?" is a script you have probably read to your parents more than once. Mom and Dad may not know exactly how to answer, but you're right about one thing: it is indeed a new generation. Nobody knows better than your parents that things are certainly different from what they used to be. But they know, too, about things that never change. God doesn't change, his Word doesn't change—so neither do his values. He makes it plain throughout the New Testament that living for Jesus Christ in a fallen world has been the same uphill battle for all of us in *every* generation. But this is a battle worth every bit of energy and determination we put into it. More often than not, it is a battle of ideas, values, and beliefs.

Those are the things most easily influenced by what we program into our mental computers.

 ## Violence and the GIGO Syndrome

There is little doubt that the sharp increase in sexual and other violent crime these days is a reflection of the GIGO syndrome. The human tragedies all around us are among the strongest reasons we ought to be careful about the way we program our minds. When people's minds are constantly stimulated with ideas of sex and violence, they have a nasty way, sooner or later, of wanting to act out those ideas. When the circumstances offer the right setting for it, some of these same people start doing what they have been programmed to do.

One thing all of us could do to stop that trend is get honest about what we can and cannot control. One of our favorite pastimes is making excuses—pleading helplessness and innocence in things we figure are beyond our control. But when we really try, we find we *can* control what TV programs we watch and what movies we see. And aren't *you* the only one who can decide which magazines to read, which records or compact discs to buy, and which videotapes to rent?

 ## The Dogfight Inside Us

An old Indian chief became a Christian many years ago. After struggling for a long time with the changes in his life, he talked about his problems with a wise minister of the gospel.

"Sometimes it seems that a white dog and black dog inside me are fighting, both very strong and fierce," the chief explained. "When white dog is winning, everything goes well. But when black dog is on top, things are very bad for me. What do you advise that chief do about this dogfight?"

"Very simple," replied the minister. "Feed only the white dog!"

That's wise advice, the reason being that we really are what we *think*. We have more control over our input than we like to admit, so work on a new pattern of making your own choices—more *careful* ones. Start feeding the white dog inside you and starving the black one. Talk to the Lord about it the next time you want to rent a videotape. When sex and violence come on the TV screen, grit your teeth and switch channels. Better yet, take your Bible someplace quiet and spend time getting better acquainted with the way God feels about your life. You'll be amazed at the difference that change of input makes in what your personal computer cranks out.

# 19

# The Unwanted Pregnancy

e've already covered the unpleasant fact that illicit and promiscuous sex can cause either partner a bad disease that could prove very distressing and uncomfortable, if not fatal. Another serious consequence of promiscuity is also a jarring surprise but reserved for the girl. That's the ever-present possibility of getting pregnant—a breathtaking discovery guaranteed to ruin any otherwise bright and sunny day.

##  An Idiotic Risk

"I could have just died!" a fifteen-year-old told me, describing the moment she got the bad news. "Sure, I had thought about the risk of getting pregnant at the time I, uh, did it with him. But maybe it's kind of like

159

playing Russian Roulette, you know. He wants you to do it, and maybe so do you. Sure, you're scared but you go ahead anyway and figure—you know—having a baby won't happen to you. But it did to me, right? And the very first time, too. Now look at the mess I'm in!"

"Playing Russian Roulette" is a good way to describe promiscuity. God's process for continuing the cycle of life on Planet Earth involves getting female eggs and male sperm together. Once that process is set in motion, "nature" takes its course. God wants our sexual urges to be more about babies and parental responsibility and respecting his guidelines than about irresponsible fun. Sure, it's a wonderful bonus that God makes sex pleasurable, but we had best not let the pleasure of it make us forget that sex involves responsibility and marital commitment.

Since sex is not meant to be fun-and-games, ignoring that particular fact of life can be an idiotic risk similar to Russian Roulette. Spin the cylinder, hope the bullet is in another chamber, put the revolver to your temple, and pull the trigger. Will it click or will it BANG?

Despite all the practical warnings and moral outcries, thousands of unwanted pregnancies happen every year. So does the pain and humiliation that goes with them. Adding to the tragedy, many of these pregnancies end in abortion, the first solution that comes to mind for some people when they discover that "something went wrong" and a baby was conceived.

 ## Abortion Is Killing

It takes moral stamina to resist that first impulse to get rid of an unwanted baby, especially since other people may be urging it. "Why not?" a seventeen-year-old asked flippantly when she talked with a school counselor about her third pregnancy. She had handled the first two by having abortions, and this one seemed no different. "It's getting to be a habit, I guess," she shrugged. To her, abortion was not much different from having a wart zapped off her hand.

Elective abortion is a medical procedure in which the living embryo or fetus is killed by dislodging it from the lining of the uterus. The baby's pitiful remains are discharged through the vagina and are often dismembered or torn apart in the process. The dead baby is not accorded the dignity of a burial. The little body probably goes into the same garbage as the bloody bandages, the appendixes, the tumors and the gallbladders.

That apparently doesn't bother the people who perform the operation; to them it's just a business. The baby is an inconvenience and/or an embarrassment for the prospective mother, and she wants to be rid of it. The abortionist's job is to kill it for her. Since it would be illegal to murder the baby after birth, the execution takes place while the baby is still an "it," being nurtured in the womb. That way the murder can be called "terminating a pregnancy," which sounds better than "murder." The clinicians usually assure the expectant mother that they perform abortions every day, with no ill effects for the women. Others will do it tomorrow, next month, and next year. They will keep on killing babies as long as humans indulge in promiscuous sex and refuse to accept responsibility for what they do.

 ## This Is "Freedom"?

Proponents of abortion argue that women should be free to do whatever they please with their own bodies.

WHEEL OF MISFORTUNE
LIKE TO TRY AGAIN?
OH NO!
PREGNANT
DISGRACE
SYPHILIS
GUILT
HERPES
AIDS

Many women have found, though, that they are not really free to make their own choice on the question of abortion. They are virtually forced by someone else to make the terrifying decision. Later they may deeply regret their hasty option to kill the fetus. Some women end up with disabling and long-term emotional scars because of that decision. Others die from loss of blood or massive infection. Abortion, like promiscuous sex, is a form of Russian Roulette.

Aborting a fetus is a medical procedure that is risky, as is *any* surgery. For the record, here are some unpleasant things that can happen to a woman who decides to get rid of the baby living in her womb:

- She can bleed to death. Many abortion patients have done so, even under the most "medically safe" conditions.
- She can suffer infection or surgical damage to the uterus or other female organs, causing considerable pain and suffering—even death.
- Infection, surgical damage, or other complications can make it impossible for her to bear children later, when she does want them.
- Her emotional ability to enjoy sex in the future or to be an adequate sex partner may be jeopardized.
- She can suffer long-range and perhaps irreversible psychological damage, due to remorse and guilt over having killed her child.

 ## Saying "No" to Murder

If you know someone who is being pressed to have an abortion, suggest a careful study of that list. Remind her that "freedom" means she is also free to say "No."

Let us downplay for a moment the danger to physical health and the emotional risk and ask whether the Bible speaks of rightness and wrongness where abortion is concerned. Is there a clear biblical principle we ought to follow here?

Yes, there is. The Sixth Commandment certainly applies: "Thou shalt not kill." Abortion clearly violates that commandment. There is never a time when a fetus is not a living organism! Think about that. Terminating a pregnancy, by whatever name we call it, means *killing* a human being, ending a life. Unusual circumstances, like rape, incest or a medical crisis, might color the ethics involved, but remember that killing a human organism is murder.

Make sure you grasp what I just said. It is based on a principle that stands on its own. Life does not really "start" except as a continuation of an ongoing process and set of conditions. If you plant a healthy but dead-looking seed in the right kind of soil and give it the right kind of care, you find it was alive all the time. Otherwise, it wouldn't produce a plant in a million years. A baby, too, even before birth, is a living organism, a continuation of something alive. Since life cannot be generated spontaneously, we cannot say at some point during a pregnancy, that "yesterday this was a dead 'thing.' But today something mystical happened and it became a person."

In essence, nobody "comes to life," since his or her existence is passed along and triggered by life forms that went before. Sure, "life" is always a mystery, but one thing is plain: it always arises as the product of an ongoing life process. Once the living egg of the mother and the living sperm of the father join to pass along the gift of life to their child, there is no intervening period of "non-life," or existence as a "thing." The mother and father do not contribute just inorganic chemicals mixed in a combination that would gradually generate life where life does not exist. No, the fetus in a womb is a continuation of aliveness. It is a merging of *living* components contributed by the mother and the father. Stopping the process robs a little *person* of his or her life.

All the arguments about when the fetus "gets a soul and becomes a person" blur the simple fact that life is not such an off-on phenomenon. Just as conceiving a child passes on the precious gift of life, abortion means that someone invades the protecting enclosure of the womb with a cold, steel instrument of death and snuffs out life.

##  A Handy New Way to Kill

In October 1988, a European drug manufacturer, Roussell-Uclaf, started selling a product it calls RU-486. This pill eliminates the need for surgical abortion because it destroys a fetus by acting on the chemistry of the mother's body. RU-486 stops the flow of progesterone to the cells in the lining of a woman's uterus. That means the uterus wall will break down the same way it does during the menstrual cycle when *no* pregnancy has occurred. The fetus is dislodged in the process and the pregnancy is terminated.

When the drug first became available, people all over the world who oppose abortion on moral grounds demanded it be taken off the market. Roussell-Uclaf decided that RU-486 was not a good idea after all and stopped selling it, but the government of France overruled that decision and insisted the pills be made available again. Now it seems that this pill and drugs similar to it will be appearing almost everywhere, legally or illegally, as one more way to handle unwanted pregnancies.

What that means is that expectant mothers who deny the sanctity of life can turn to RU-486 and its clones as a handy means of self-administered "abortion." To them, getting rid of the new life created through promiscuous sex will become no big deal. They will consider it a minor nuisance no worse than ridding their bodies of an intestinal parasite or a colony of Asian flu viruses.

At least RU-486 serves to make the true issue more clear. For Christians, the real objection to abortion is not the risk and horror of the mechanical or surgical means by which it is done. Abortion—whether by pill or by vacuum aspirator—kills a human who has the right to live. Abortion is murder, and God has commanded us "Thou shalt not kill."

 ## Plenty of Alternatives

But what are the alternatives to aborting an unwanted pregnancy? There are some acceptable ones. For one thing, if the father and mother are mature enough and love each other, marriage can be an option. Never mind the old jokes about "shotgun marriages." The key questions are concerned with whether the two youngsters love and respect each other. If they do, are they willing to learn and profit from their mistake and get on with their lives? Do they want the little person they are bringing into the world to grow up in the best possible environment—with both mother and father? If the answers are "Yes," they should try to find a way to overcome the practical obstacles, get married, and settle down to the task of raising their family. Perhaps their parents will help. Of course, getting married at a young age will change life for them considerably, but they were vested with a certain responsibility when they conceived the child. With the right kind of love as a foundation, marriage might give their baby the best chance of developing into a happy and useful human being.

But there are other alternatives as well. Sometimes, when marriage to the baby's father is not feasible or desired by *both* young people, a young unwed mother's parents have taken her baby and raised it as their own. Or grandparents might agree to provide the parental care the child will need until the mother can establish a home of her own. If such options are impossible, the mother might join the growing ranks of "parents without partners" and raise the child single-handedly. That takes courage and is often neither a practical nor the most promising solution. But it can be done.

Hundreds of Christian ministries across our nation provide loving prenatal care for unwed mothers. This includes lodging, counseling, help with medical care, fellowship of others in the same predicament, and opportunities to learn the Word of God and grow spiritually.

These same ministries can also arrange for adoption. If the mother and father are in full agreement that this is the right solution for everyone, adoption can frequently be a good alternative and best for all concerned. The baby can be placed with a reputable Christian family that will love it and raise it as its own. Ties with the birth mother can be maintained if that is agreeable to everybody, but a clean break can be made if that seems best. That break can be a sad one, but it does not compare with the guilt and shame experienced by mothers who order the execution of a baby still in the womb.

 ## What Is God's Role?

This seems as good a place as any to wonder again, "What is God's role in this matter of sex?" If we could compare our Creator with any human, it would be as an inventor and designer. He knows infinitely better than we do how his creation must function for the greatest enjoyment and maximum benefits. He knows the frightful mistakes people can make when his authority is rejected. What God is saying to us—and what this book is saying—is, "Look, I know how this thing works best, and I'm on your side. I can forgive you and help you when you fail. But look at the directions before you take an impulsive leap and mess it up for yourself!"

Another way to word God's message is this: "Don't live by your glands; live by faith and by my commandments. Use the brains I've given you. Make things right when you fail. Never doubt that I love you and know what I'm doing."

There is more to boy/girl love than stimulated nerve endings sneaked in the back seat of a car, on the beach, under a bush, or on a couch in the basement. God has provided us with bright ideals that will never change until he changes—and he is not going to! Faithfulness to those ideals ensures our personal peace. We can inherit a dismal personal world, though, by letting them slip carelessly through our fingers.

# 20

# Life on a Turkey Farm

Sometimes it seems as if the talent we humans exhibit most often is our unique ability to mess things up. Of course, we're inclined to notice that foul-it-up ability in others before we acknowledge it in ourselves. Whether we admit it or not, we are the biggest part of the problem. Sooner or later, if we're honest with ourselves, we get around to recognizing that we are neither geniuses nor saints. Each of us is flawed to some degree.

 ## Two Important Discoveries

With that introduction in mind, let me share with you a couple of important discoveries all humans must make if we want to handle the complications of life on

Planet Earth. I hope you will commit to memory what I modestly call Watson's Observations:

- **Important Discovery Number One:** The world is a gigantic turkey farm.
- **Important Discovery Number Two:** One of the turkeys is *me*!

You may have to ponder those little gems for a while before they sink in and lights begin to flash in your brain. If you stick with Watson's Observations long enough, though, I think you'll get the point. With those two principles firmly established, you'll be able to relax a little and enjoy life more.

Not that there's anything new about those observations. It should be obvious that they are really not discoveries, because they are a modern-day restatement of a Bible truth: ". . . all have sinned and fall short of the glory of God . . ." (Rom. 3:23). "All" includes *you* and *me,* of course. That means it makes no sense to go through life trying to blame "those other guys" every time things go wrong. We need to get busy doing something about our own flaws before we complain about all the other turkeys out there who insist on messing up the farm.

 ## You Should Have Said "No"

Maybe you have not yet discovered that messing up is a widespread human failure that affects *all* of us. If not, you ought to take a closer look at some of your own recent boo-boos. My guess is some of them resulted in consequences you would be glad to do without.

Like the times, maybe, when you could have said "no," but didn't. In spite of your better judgment and the proddings of your conscience, you gave in and said "yes"—or even "maybe." Remember? And the result of that particular kind of foolishness can hurt a lot, as you probably know. It can go all the way from embarrassment or guilt trips that won't quit to painful and costly problems with parents, friends, school authorities, *and* yourself. Maybe it even involves a problem with the law.

And since you're a Christian—be honest now—didn't the last time you didn't say "no" (when you should have) also involve a certain amount of hiding from God? Did you hope he wasn't looking when things got out of control? Would you like a second shot at some of those dumb decisions to prove you could do it better next time? Well, one of the really neat things we learn from the Bible about God is that he is always willing to give us another chance. That's what grace is all about—we are forgiven, even though we don't deserve it.

 ## Four Christian "Can-Dos"

As a Christian, you might get some helpful ideas from four simple rules for being a winner in handling all your problems, including sex. All four of those rules fall easily into your realm of "can-dos." Are you ready? Here they are:

- Remember that God really knows and cares.
- Insist on getting the facts.
- Take the initiative.
- Stay in control.

One reason those are helpful guidelines is that if you take the four reminders apart and look at them under a microscope, you find that they address the fact that we ourselves are at the root of most of *all* our human problems.

But let's zoom the microscope in a little closer on those four Christian "can-dos."

1. *Affirming your faith.* Any time a Christian messes up through disobedience and rebellion, it involves a denial of everything that is supposed to be important about God. Such a foul-up contradicts what we say we believe about Jesus, the Bible, our values, and our faith. By the way, trying to lose weight always reminds me of that truth. When I'm attempting to shed pounds, I sometimes mess up my diet by sneaking stuff out of the refrigerator behind my wife's back. It's as if I think the calories won't count if Diane doesn't catch me. It takes the bathroom scales to bring me back to painful reality.

If we drop our standards and renounce our values even for a minute, we are implying that God either doesn't know or doesn't care and thus that our sin doesn't count. He *knows,* of course, because he is the all-knowing God, and he proved how much he *cares* when He sent his Son to die for our sins. Sooner or later, the painful consequences of our rebellion will jerk us back to reality.

2. *Getting the facts.* An awful lot of our problems can be avoided if we take the time to get the facts—learn the truth—before we get involved. That's really what a sex education book is all about: getting the facts. That includes Bible facts as well as biological know-how.

When you have gotten in trouble, do you lower your head and mumble, "I didn't think" (or "I didn't realize"

or "I didn't know")? All of us often do. But is that a legitimate excuse? How much better things would have been if we *had* thought—and realized and known—before the trouble began. Armed with the truth, you have a lot better chance to be a winner.

3. *Being the leader.* I asked a sharp teenager once if he knew what "take the initiative," means and he answered, "Sure, it means being the one who starts things." He was right on target, but there's another side to its meaning that you can't afford to overlook. You see, taking the initiative sometimes means *stopping* things before they get out of hand.

Are you somebody who starts and stops things? If you are, you're a leadership type. You refuse to be like the proverbial lamb led to the slaughter. True, that's the Old Testament model of what happened to Jesus when he took our place and died for our sins. But Jesus did this *voluntarily* because he was God and was intervening to save us. When trouble threatens, try being the one who *starts* things going in the right direction or *stops* them from taking the wrong one, depending on what is needed. People who take the initiative are the ones who not only choose the direction in which their own lives move but also now and then guide the lives of others as well. They first decide what *ought* to be done or not done—what makes sense on the basis of the facts and God's purposes—and they take the initiative in doing it right.

4. *Staying in control.* "I don't know; it just seemed like I lost control," a tearful teenage girl told me. She was attempting to explain how she got into a real messy problem she was trying hard to resolve. As everyone knows, losing control is not all that hard to do.

But neither is *keeping* control, once you've decided what makes sense and what it takes to be a winner.

The way to stay in control is to be especially alert and determined when things threaten to get out of hand. If you're honest with yourself, you can usually tell when trouble is brewing, and right then you can do something about it. Because God really is there, knowing and caring, you can be sure he will help you get things back on track.

You can do that by using your head, not your feelings. Remember, in your head—your thinking—is where your values and your commitment are written. And that's what determines who you really are.

##  Calling the Signals

If you don't call your own signals, someone else will call them for you. And when another human calls the signals, especially if he or she doesn't have your convictions, it often spells trouble. That's particularly true in matters of sex. When it's too late to undo the damage caused by promiscuity, the consequences for the person who wimps out can be painful and costly to live with.

But never forget that it's not too late right now to start over again, if starting over is what you need. Once you get the facts—the inside information on what God tells us about himself in the Bible—we know he freely forgives, heals, and restores. But we have to ask for it. When we do, forgiveness, healing, and restoration are ours. It matters not how far down the wrong road you have gone before realizing that God means what he says and keeps all his promises.

So, if reconciliation with God is what you need . . . well, he's the only One who can give it. That means he's the One you probably ought to talk it over with right now.